MASONRY

REVEALED AND ILLUSTRATED,

WITH A SKETCH OF THE

LIFE, ABDUCTION AND MURDER

OF

WILLIAM MORGAN.

PUBLISHED BY MATTHEW GARDINER,

AND FOR SALE BY BOOKSELLERS GENERALLY.

CATALOGUE OF POPULAR BOOKS

RECENTLY PUBLISHED

FOR THE TRADE,

By Lorenzo Stratton, No. 131 Main St., Cincinnati, Ohio.

The Female Spy, or Treason in Camp—
  by Emerson Bennett 25
Rosalie Du Pont, a sequel to the Female
  Spy—by Emerson Bennett 25
The Traitor, or Fate of Ambition, 2 vols.
  by Emerson Bennett 50
Bandits of the Osage—by E. Bennett ... 25
The Unknown Countess—by E. Bennett. 25
League of the Miami—by E. Bennett ... 25
Oliver Goldfinch, or The Hypocrite—by
  Emerson Bennett 25
Kate Clarendon—by Emerson Bennett ... 25

SELECT WORKS OF G. P. R. JAMES.
The Belle of the Court, or One in a
  Thousand 25
Count De Castelneu 25
Philip Augustus 25
Mary of Burgundy 25
Gentleman of the Old School 25
Richelieu 25
The Collegians 25

SELECT WORKS OF EUGENE SUE.
The Princess of Hansfield 25
Louise De Villiers 25
The Duchess Almeda 25
The Commander of Malta 25
Anthony the Brigand—by Dumas 25
The Fencing-master—by Dumas 25
Zanoni—by Sir E. L. Bulwer 25
Godolphin—by Sir E. L. Bulwer 25
The Money Lender—by Mrs. Gore 25
The Trapper's Bride—by the author of
  Prairie Bird 25

Madeline O'Moore—by Charles Lever. 25
Life of Dr. Jennings, The Victimizer.... 25
The Man of Enterprise—by J. A. Sperry. 25
The Lily of Sonora—by C. G. Chipman . 25
Tales of Lake Caddo 25
Misfortunes of Teddy O'Bryan 25
Grace Willoughby—by the author of
  Hector O'Halloran 50
History of the Cuban Expedition 25
Ellen Winston—by Walter Whitmore... 25

THE SELECT WORKS OF CHARLES DICKENS.
The Pickwick Club ....
Nicholas Nickleby ....
Oliver Twist ....
The Housekeeper's Book—by Mrs. S. J.
  Stratton ....
The Farmer and Gardener, or Book of
  the Seasons—by A. Randall ....
New Testament, School Edition .....
The Masonic Institution—by John
  Adams. Muslin, 1.25. Paper ....
Journal of Correspondence b
  Lor   ron and the Countess
  s   oth, 75. Paper .....
P   e. 50 Colored
           —by More
Co   Far
New   te
America
The Negro
The Complete
BOOK ....

LORENZO STRA

as also on hand, and can supply, every variety of
  rican and English standard Poets, at wholesale a
  ters for all the Magazines and Periodical pu'
  eru cash prices. Orders by Mail, Railroad, St
  ded to. Single copies of the above list can
  closing the amount, post paid, directed to
                LORENZ

s. Gift Books, Annuals,
  ablishment is also head-
  e furnishes at the lowest
  on Lines, will be promptly
  il to any post of the U. S. A.,
  .31 Main Street, Cincinnati, O.

ILLUSTRATIONS

OF

MASONRY,

BY ONE OF THE FRATERNITY,

WHO HAS DEVOTED THIRTY YEARS TO THE SUBJECT:

WITH AN APPENDIX,

CONTAINING

A KEY

TO THE HIGHER DEGREES OF

FREEMASONRY;

BY A MEMBER OF THE CRAFT.

CINCINNATI:
PUBLISHED BY MATTHEW GARDINER

NORTHERN DISTRICT OF NEW YORK, TO WIT:

BE IT REMEMBERED, That on the fourteenth day of August, in the fifty-first year of the independence of the United States of America, A. D. 1826, WILLIAM MORGAN, of the said district, hath deposited in this office the title of a book, the right whereof, he claims as author, in the words following, to wit:

" Illustrations of Masonry, by one of the fraternity, who has devoted thirty years to the subject. 'God said, let there be light, and there was light.' "

In conformity to the act of Congress of the United States, entitled " An act for the encouragement of learning, by securing the copies of maps, charts, and books, to the authors and proprietors of such copies, during the times therein mentioned;" and also to the act entitled " an act supplementary to the act entitled ' an act for the encouragement of learning, by securing the copies of maps, charts and books, to the authors and proprietors of such copies, during the times therein mentioned,' and extending the benefits thereof to the arts of designing, engraving, and etching historical and other prints."

R. R. LANSING,
Clerk of the Northern District of New York.

INTRODUCTION.

In the absence of the author, or rather compiler of the following work, who was kidnapped and carried away from the village of Batavia, on the 11th day of September, 1826, by a number of Freemasons, it devolves upon the publisher to attempt to set forth some of the leading views that governed those who embarked in the undertaking.

To contend with prejudice, and to struggle against customs and opinions, which superstition, time, and ignorance have hallowed, requires time, patience, and magnanimity. When we begin to pull down the strong-holds of error, the batteries we level against them, though strong and powerful and victorious at last, are at first received with violence; and when in our conquering career we meet with scoffs and revilings from the besieging partisans of untenable positions, it the more forcibly impresses us, we are but men; and that in every work of reformation and renovation we must encounter various difficulties. For a full confirmation of our statement we might refer to the history of the world. It is not our intention however, to give a full detail of the *whims* and *caprices* of man—to bring forth the historic records of other years as proofs of the windings and shiftings of the various characters who have "Strutted their brief hour on life's stage," in order to convince, that customs, associations, and institutions are like the lives of the authors and abettors, fleeting and fragile. Many of them rise up as bubbles on the ocean, and die away. Circumstances give them existence, and when these causes cease to exist, they go into the same gulf of oblivion as countless exploded opinions and tenets have gone before them. The mind that formed and planned them goes on in its dazzling flight, bounding over barrier after barrier, until it has arrived at the ultimate goal of consummation.

The daily occurrences before us bring forth the full conviction, that the emanation from the God of light is gradually ascending to regions of greater intellectual brilliancy.

When we view man, in the infancy of society, as in the childhood of his existence, he is weak, powerless, and defenseless; but in his manhood and riper years, he has grown to his full stature, and stands forth in commanding attitude, the favored and acknowledged lord of the world. For his comfort and well-being, as a member of society, rules and regulations are necessary. In the various stages of his progress, these systematic improvements undergo various changes, according to circumstances and situations.—What is proper and necessary in one grade of society, is wholly useless, and may be alarming in another. Opinions and usages, that go down in tradition, and interfere not with our improvements in social concerns, adhere to us more closely, and become entwined in all our feelings. It is to this we owe our bigoted attachment to antiquity—it is this that demands from us a superstitious reverence for the opinions and practices of men of former times, and closes the ear against truth, and blinds the eyes to the glare of new light and new accessions of knowledge; through which medium only can they break in upon the mind.

We have within ourselves the knowledge, and everywhere around us the proofs that we are beings destined not to *stand* still. In our present state of advancement, we look with pity on the small progress of our Fathers in arts and sciences, and social institutions; and when compared with our elevated rank, we have just cause of pride and of grateful feelings. —They did well for the times in which they lived, but to the ultimatum of perfectibility we are nearer—and in the monuments we have before us of the skill and genius of our times and age, we have only fulfilled those destinies for which we were created; and we object to every obstacle that opposes or attempts to oppose the will of Heaven.

In the present enlightened state, to which society has advanced we contend that the opinions and tenets, and pretended secrecies of "olden times," handed down to us, should be fully, fairly and freely canvassed; that from the mist and darkness which have hung over them, they should come out before the open light of day, and be subjected to the rigid test of candid investigation. These preliminary remarks lead us to the main object of our introduction.

We come to lay before the world the claims of an institution which has been sanctioned by ages, venerated for wisdom, and exalted for 'light;' but, an institution whose benefits have always been overrated, and whose continuance is not, in the slightest degree, necessary. We meet it with its high requirements, its "time-honored customs," its swelling titles, and shall show it in its nakedness and simplicity. Strip it of its "borrowed trappings" and it is a *mere nothing*—a toy not now worthy the notice of a child to sport with. We look back to it as, at one period, a "cement of society, and bond of union."—We view it as, at one time, a venerable fort,—but now in ruins —which contained within its walls many things that dignified and adorned human nature. We give it due credit for the services it has done; but at present, when light has gone abroad into the uttermost recesses and corners of the world—when information is scattered wide around us, and knowledge is not closeted in cloisters and cells but "stalks abroad with her beams of

INTRODUCTION.

light, and her honors and rewards," we may now, when our minority has expired, act up to our character, and look no longer to Masonry as our guide and conductor: it has nothing in it now valuable that is not known to every inquiring mind: it contains, wrapped up in its supposed mysteries, no useful truth, no necessary knowledge, that has not gone forth to the world through other channels and by other means. If we would have a knowledge of sacred history—of the religion and practices of the Jews, and the terms and technicalities of the Mosaic institution, we can have recourse to the Bible. If we wish further communications from Heaven, we have open to our view the pages of the New Testament. If we would "climb the high ascent of human science, and trace the mighty progress of human genius in every gigantic effort of mind, in logic, geometry, mathematics, chemistry, and every other branch of knowledge," we ridicule the idea that Masonry, in her retirements, contains the arts and sciences. The sturdiest Mason in the whole fraternity is not bold enough to uphold or maintain the opinion, for one moment, in sober reality. The origin of the institution is easily traced to the rude ages of the world,—to a body of mechanics, or a corporation of operative workmen who formed signs and regulations, the more easily to carry on their work, and to protect their order. (The very obligations solemnly rendered to every member, carry the strongest internal evidence of the semi-barbarity that prevailed at the time of the institution of the order.) In the course of time, as society increased, and knowledge became more general, it spread, and embracing in its grasp other objects than at first, it enrolled in its ranks men of the first respectability in wealth, talents, and worth. But that there is anything intrinsically valuable in the signs, symbols, or words of Masonry no man of sense will contend. That there is any hidden secret which operates as a talismanic charm on its possessors, every man of intelligence, Mason or no Mason, must candidly acknowledge. It is worse than idleness for the defenders of the order, at the present day, to intrench themselves behind their outward show—the semblance before the world—and to say *they are in possession of superior knowledge.*

We pretend not to act under a cover. We shall 'tell the truth, the whole truth, and nothing but the truth.' Masonry, it is true, has long been eulogized in songs—it has formed the burden of the poet's theme, and been the subject of the orator's best performances. Fancy has been almost exhausted in bringing out 'new flowers to deck the fairy queen;' but when we come behind the scenes, what is the picture we behold! Are we to rest satisfied with the *ipse dixit* of others, or to examine the truth for ourselves? The touchstone is before our readers in the present publication

Masonry is, of itself, naked and worthless. It consists of gleanings from the Holy Scriptures, and from the arts and sciences, which have shone in the world. Linking itself with philosophy, and science, and religion, on this it

INTRODUCTION.

rests all its claims to veneration and respect. Take away this borrowed aid, and it falls into ruins.

Much weight is still attached to the argument, that as a tie uniting men—that, as a significant speech, symbolically speaking every language, and at the same time embodying in its constitution everything that is valuable, it should command respect. We meet this argument with facts that cannot be controverted. We put it on a basis that will fling into the back-ground every quibble and artifice on the subject; and, in the language of a polemic writer, we challenge opposition to our position:—

'The religion inculcated by the Son of Man does all this; and in no possible situation can man be placed, that the benign influence of Christianity does not completely supersede the use of a mere human institution. Place a brother in a desert, unfriended and unknown,—leave him in a wilderness where human footsteps never printed the ground, the Divine Benefactor is at his side, and watches over him with parental guidance. Let him be driven on a barbarous coast in the midst of savage men, and there it is that the breathings of the divine influence spreads around him its shield; bring him into civilized society—in the busy walks of men, and are we to be told that as members of community, sojourners on earth, and candidates for heaven, we must be taught our duty at a Mason's Lodge? Wherever Masonry exercises its influence with success, there Christianity can have, or should have, a more powerful effect. Whenever Masonry claims 'kindred with the skies,' and exalts herself above every living sublunary thing, then, with an unhallowed step, it obtrudes on the sacred borders of religion, and 'decks itself in borrowed garments.'

Intrenched within these strong walls—decked with all the glitter of high-sounding professions, claiming what does not belong to it,—it dazzles 'but to bewilder and destroy.' In its train, in these United States, are enrolled many periodical works devoted to Masonry; and, under the guise of patronizing mechanics—the arts and sciences lend their aid to carry on the imposing delusion. They take up the specious title of throwing a little illumination on this benighted country, from their secret depositories. Arrogating to itself what should deck others' brows—assuming to be the patron, the life and soul of all that is great and valuable—it deceives many of its votaries, and from its *gaudy* premises the most untenable and erroneous conclusions are drawn.

Are we astonished at the wild and heedless manner in which many of the votaries of Masonry rush into every excess—putting at defiance the laws of our civil institutions, which suffer no one to be put in jeopardy but by due forms, and disregarding the command of the Most High, which says, thou shalt not kill!—we can readily trace the cause to the impressions and practices obtained from its false tenets and deceptive arrogance. Masonry is to the modern world what the whore of Babylon was to the ancient; and is the beast with seven heads and ten horns, ready to tear out our bowels, and *scatter them to the four winds of heaven.*

Masonry gives rogues and evil-minded characters an opportunity of visiting upon their devoted victim, all the ills attending combined power, when exerted to accomplish destruction. It works unseen, at all silent hours, and secret times and places; and like *death,* when summoning his diseases, pounces upon its devoted subject, and lays him prostrate in the dust. Like the great enemy of man, it has shown its cloven foot, and put the public upon its guard against its secret machinations.

This part of the subject requires no further discussion either by way of ridicule or downright sincerity, but the remark, which cannot be too often reiterated, that the world, in its present advanced state, requires no such order for our social intercourse; and when the masonic mania prevails as it now does in this country, we are exalting a mere human ordinance, with its useless trumpery and laughable accompaniments for the sublime and unadorned lessons of Heaven.

To some men it is galling and mortifying in the extreme to give up their darling systems. With the increase of years their fondness becomes so great that they cling to them with wild and bewildered attachment.—But we would ask them where now are the Knights of Malta and Jerusalem, and the objects that called forth their peril and journeyings? Where are the crusades and excursions on which our grand Commanders, Generalissimos and Sir Knights are to be engaged...........In no other excursions than Cervantes describes of his redoubtable Hero, *Don Quixotte.* The days and occasions that called forth these deeds of chivalry and valor have passed like those before the flood; and the *mock* dignitaries and *Puppet-show* actions of Masons in their imitation call forth pity and indignation. When we now see the gaudy show in a Lodge-room, and a train of nominal officers with their distinctions and badges, it may give us some faint idea of scenes that are past, and may gratify an idle curiosity, but produce no substantial good under heaven. When monasteries and cloisters, and Inquisitor's cells and prisons have been broken up before the sweeping march of the moral mind, why this unnecessary mummery should be so much countenanced in this country, above all other countries in the world, is a matter of astonishment.

The day, we trust, will never arrive here, when ranks in Masonry will be stepping-stones to places of dignity and power—when this institution will be a machine to press down the free-born spirit of men. We have now no tyrant to rule over us—no kingly potentate to move over our heads the rod of authority; but high in our elevation, and invincible in our strongholds, we put at defiance secret cabals and associations. The public opinion is like a mighty river, and gigantic in its course, it will sweep every interposing obstacle before it.

In the work which we submit to the public we have given false coloring to nothing: nor in these remarks have we set down aught in malice. In the firm discharge of our undertaking we have been stern and unbending as the rugged mountain oak: and persecutions, pains, and perils have not deterred us from our purpose. We have triumphed over tumult, and clamor, and evil-speaking.

When our book goes out to the world, it will meet with attacks of a violent nature from one source, and men of mock titles and order will endeavor to heap upon it every calumny. Men more tenacious of absolute forms and practice than they are attentive to truth and honor, will deny our expositions, and call us Liars and Impostors.

Such is the treatment, however ungenerous and unjust, which we expect to meet, and for which we are prepared. Truth, we know, is majestic and will finally prevail. The little petty effusions of malice that will be thrown out will die with their authors, whom this work will survive.

We now aver, in defiance of whatever may be said to the contrary—no matter by whom, however exalted his rank—that this Book is what it pretends to be—that it is a Master Key to the secrets of Masonry; that in the pages before him, the man of candor and inquiry can judge for himself, and then a proper judgment will be formed of our intention.

ILLUSTRATIONS OF MASONRY, ETC.

A DESCRIPTION of the ceremonies used in opening a Lodge of Entered Apprentice Masons; which is the same in all the upper degrees, with the exception of the difference in the signs, due-guards, grips, pass-grips, words and their several names; all of which will be given and explained in their proper places as the work progresses

One rap calls the Lodge to order—one calls up the Junior and Senior Deacons—two raps call up all the subordinate officers, and three all the members of the Lodge.

The Master having called the Lodge to order, and the officers all seated, the Master says to the Junior Warden, 'Brother Junior, are they all Entered Apprentice Masons in the South?' *Ans.* 'They are, Worshipful.' Master to the Senior Warden, 'Brother Senior, are they all Entered Apprentice Masons in the West?' *Ans.* 'They are, Worshipful.' The Master then says, 'They are, in the East,' at the same time he gives a rap with the common gavel or mallet, which calls up both Deacons. Master to Junior Deacon, 'Brother Junior, the first care of a Mason?' *Ans.* 'To see the Lodge Tyled, Worshipful.' Master to Junior Deacon. 'Attend to that part of your duty, and inform the Tyler that we are about to open a lodge of Entered Apprentice Masons, and direct him to tyle accordingly.' The Tyler then steps to the door and gives three raps, which are answered by three from without; The Junior Deacon then gives one, which is also answered by the Tyler with one; the door is then partly opened, and the Junior Deacon delivers his message, and resumes his situation, and says, 'the door is tyled, Worshipful,' (at the same time giving the due-guard, which is never omitted when the master is addressed). The Master to the Junior Deacon, 'By whom?' *Ans.* 'By a Master Mason without the door, armed with the proper implement of his office.' Master to Junior Deacon, 'His duty there?' *Ans.* 'To keep off all cowans and eaves-droppers, see that none pass or repass without permission from the Master.' [Some say, without permission from the chair.] Master to Junior Deacon, 'Brother Junior your place in the lodge?' *Ans.* 'At the right-hand of the Senior Warden in the West.' Master to Junior Deacon, 'Your business there, Brother Junior?' *Ans.* 'To wait on the Worshipful Master and Wardens, act as their proxy in the active duties of the Lodge, and take charge of the door.' Master to Junior Deacon, 'The Senior Deacon's place in the Lodge?' *Ans.* 'At the right hand of the Worshipful Master in the East.' (The Master while asking the last question, gives two raps, which call up all the subordinate officers.) Master to Senior Deacon, 'Your duty there, Brother Senior?' *Ans.* 'To wait on the Worshipful Master and Wardens, act as their proxy in the active duties of the Lodge, attend to the preparation and introduction of candidates, and welcome and clothe all visiting brethren, (i e. furnish them with an apron). Master to Senior eacon, 'The Secretary's place in the Lodge, Brother Senior?' *Ans.* 'At the left-hand of the Worshipful Master in the East.' Master to Secretary, 'Your duty there, Brother Secretary?' *Ans.* 'The better to observe the Worshipful Master's will and pleasure, record the proceedings of the Lodge; transmit a copy of the same to the Grand Lodge, if required; receive all moneys and money bills from the hands of the Brethren, pay them over to the Treasurer, and take his receipt for the same.' The Master to the Secretary,'The Treasurer's place in the Lodge?' *Ans.* 'At the right-hand of the Worshipful Master.' Master to the Treasurer, 'Your duty there, Brother Treasurer?' *Ans.* 'Duly to observe the Worshipful master's will and pleasure; receive all moneys and money bills from the hands of the Secretary; keep a just and true account of the same; pay them out by order of the Worshipful Master, and consent of the Brethren.' The Master to the Treasurer, 'The Junior Warden's place in the Lodge, Brother treasurer?' *Ans.* 'In the South, Worshipful.' Master to Junior Warden, 'Your business there, Brother Junior?' *Ans.* 'As the sun in the South at high meridian is the beauty and glory of the day, so stands the Junior Warden in the South, the better to observe the time, call the crafts from labor to refreshment, superintend them during the time thereof, see that none convert the hours of refreshment into that of intemperance or excess; and call them on again in due season, that the Worshipful Master may have honor, and they pleasure and profit thereby.' Master to the Junior Warden, ' The Senior Warden's place in the Lodge?' *Ans.* ' In the West, Worshipful?' Master to Senior Warden, 'Your duty there, Brother Senior?' *Ans.* ' As the sun sets in the West to close the day, so stands the Senior Warden in the West to assist the Worshipful Master in opening his Lodge, take care of the jewels and implements, see that none be lost, pay the crafts their wages, if any be due, and see that none go away dissatisfied.' Master to the Senior Warden, ' The Master's place in the Lodge ?' *Ans.* ' In the East, Worshipful.' Master to the Senior Warden, 'His duty there ?' *Ans.* ' As the sun rises in the East to open and adorn the day, so presides the Worshipful Master in the East to open and adorn his lodge, set his crafts to work with good and wholesome laws, or cause the same to be done.' The Master now gives three raps, when all the brethren rise, and the Master taking off his hat proceeds as follows: ' In like manner, so do I, strictly forbidding all profane language, private committees, or any other disorderly conduct, whereby the peace and harmony of this Lodge may be interrupted while engaged in its lawful pursuits, under no less penalty than the bye-laws or such penalty as a majority of the brethren present may see fit to inflict. Brethren, attend to giving the signs.' (Here lodges differ very much. In some, they declare the lodge opened as follows, before they give the signs): The Master (all the Brethren imitating him) extends his left arm from his body so as to form an angle of about forty-five degrees, and holds his right hand transversely across his left, the palms thereof about one inch apart. This is called the first sign of a Mason—is the sign of distress in this degree, and alludes to the position a candidate's hands are placed in when he takes the obligation of an Entered Apprentice Mason. The Master then draws his right-hand across his throat, the hand open, with the thumb next to the throat, and drops it down by his side. This is called the due-guard of an Entered Apprentice Mason (many call it the sign), and alludes to the penalty of the obligation. (See Obligation.) The Master then declares the Lodge opened, in the following manner: 'I now declare this lodge of Entered Apprentice Masons duly opened for the dispatch of business.' The Senior Warden declares it to the Junior Warden, and he to the Brethren. Come, Brethren, let us pray. One of the following prayers is used :

Most holy and glorious God! the great Architect of the Universe; the giver of all good gifts and graces: Thou hast promised that "Where two or three are gathered together in thy name, thou wilt be in the midst of them, and bless them." In thy name we assemble, most humbly beseeching thee to bless us in all our undertakings; that we may know and serve thee aright, and that all our actions may tend to thy glory and our advancement in knowledge and virtue. And we beseech thee, O Lord God, to bless our present assembling; and to illuminate our minds through the influence of the Son of Righteousness, that we may walk in the light of thy countenance; and when the trials of our probationary state are over, be admitted into the Temple not made with hands, eternal in the heavens. Amen. So mote it be.

Another prayer, as often used at opening as closing.

Behold how good and how pleasant it is for brethren to dwell together in unity: it is like the precious ointment upon the head, that ran down upon the beard, even Aaron's beard, that went down to the skirts of his garment: as the dew of Hermon, and as the dew that descended upon the mountains of Zion, for there the Lord commanded the blessing, even life for evermore. Amen. So mote it be.

The lodge being now open and ready to proceed to business, the Master directs the Secretary to read the minutes of the last meeting which naturally brings to view the business of the present.

If there are any candidates to be brought forward, that will be the first business attended to. I will therefore proceed with a description of the ceremonies used in the admission and initiation of a candidate into the first degree of masonry.

A person wishing to become a Mason must get some one who is a Mason to present his petition to a lodge, when, if there are no serious objections, it will be entered on the minutes, and a committee of two or three appointed to inquire into his character, and report to the next regular communication. The following is the form of a petition used by a candidate; but a worthy candidate will not be rejected for the want of formality in his petition.

To the Worshipful Master Wardens and Brethren of Lodge No. —, of Free and Accepted Masons.

The subscriber, residing in ———, of lawful age, and by occupation a ———, begs leave to state that, unbiased by friends, and uninfluenced by mercenary motives, he freely and voluntarily offers himself a candidate for the mysteries of Masonry, and that he is prompted to solicit this privilege by a favorable opinion conceived of the institution, a desire of knowledge and sincere wish of being serviceable to his fellow-creatures. Should his petition be granted, he will cheerfully conform to all the ancient established usages and customs of the fraternity.

(Signed)   A. B.

At the next regular communication (if no serious objection appears against the candidate), the ballot-boxes will be passed; one black ball will reject a candidate. The boxes may be passed three times. The Deacons are the proper persons to pass them; one of the boxes has black and white beans, or balls in it, the other empty; the one with the balls in it goes before, and furnishes each member with a black and white ball; the empty box follows and receives them. There are two holes in the top of this box with a small tube (generally), in each, one of which is black, and the other white, with a partition in the box. The members put both their balls into this box as their feelings dictate; when the balls are received, the box is presented to the Master, Senior and Junior Wardens, who pronounce clear or not clear, as the case may be. The ballot proving clear, the Candidate (if present) is conducted into a small preparation room adjoining the Lodge, when he is asked the following questions, and gives the following answers. Senior Deacon to Candidate, 'Do you sincerely declare, upon your honor before these gentlemen, that unbiased by friends, uninfluenced by unworthy motives, you freely and voluntarily offer yourself a Candidate for the mysteries of masonry?' *Ans.* 'I do.' Senior Deacon to Candidate, 'Do you sincerely declare upon your honor before these gentlemen, that you are prompted to solicit the privileges of masonry, by a favorable opinion conceived of the institution, a desire of knowledge, and a sincere wish of being serviceable to your fellow creatures?' *Ans.* 'I do.' Senior Deacon to Candidate, 'Do you sincerely declare upon your honor before these gentlemen, that you will cheerfully conform to all the ancient established usages and customs of the Fraternity?' *Ans.* 'I do.' After the above questions are proposed and answered, and the result reported to the Master, he says. 'Brethren, at the request of Mr. A. B., he has been proposed and accepted in regular form. I therefore recommend him as a proper Candidate for the mysteries of Masonry, and worthy to partake of the privileges of the Fraternity: and in consequence of a declaration of his intentions, voluntarily made, I believe he will cheerfully conform to the rules of the Order.' The Candidate, during the time, is divested of all his apparel (shirt excepted), and furnished with a pair of drawers kept in the Lodge for the use of Candidates; the Candidate is then blindfolded, his left foot bare, his right in a slipper, his left breast and arm naked, and a rope, called a Cable-Tow, placed round his neck and left arm (the rope is not put round the arm in all Lodges), in which posture the Candidate is conducted to the door, where he is caused to give, or the Conductor gives, three distinct knocks, which are answered by three from within, the conductor gives one more, which is also answered by one from within. The door is then partly opened and the Junior Deacon generally asks, 'Who comes there? who comes there? who comes there?' Then the conductor, alias the Senior Deacon, answers, 'A poor blind Candidate who has long been desirous of having and receiving a part of the rights and benefits of this worshipful Lodge dedicated (some say erected) to God and held forth to the holy Order of St. John, as all true fellows and brothers have done, who have gone this way before him.' The Junior Deacon then asks, 'Is it of his own free will and accord he makes this request? is he duly and truly prepared? worthy and well qualified? and properly avouched for?' All of which being answered in the affirmative, the Junior Deacon to Senior Deacon; 'By what further rights does he expect to obtain this benefit?' *Ans.* 'By being a man, free born, of lawful age, and under the tongue of good report.' The Junior Deacon then says, 'Since this is the case you will wait till the Worshipful Master in the East is made acquainted with his request, and the answer returned.' The Junior Deacon repairs to the Master, when the same questions are asked, and answers are returned as at the door; after which, the Master says, 'Since he comes endowed with all these necessary qualifications, let him enter this Worshipful Lodge in the name of the Lord, and take heed on what he enters.' The Candidate then enters, the Junior Deacon at the same time pressing his naked left breast with the point of the compass, and asks the Candidate, 'Did you feel anything?' *Ans.* 'I Did.' Junior Deacon to Candidate, 'What was it?' *Ans.* 'A torture.' The Junior Deacon then says, 'As this is a torture to your flesh, so may it ever be to your mind and conscience if ever you should attempt to reveal the secrets of Masonry unlawfully.' The Candidate is then conducted to the center of the Lodge, where he and the Senior Deacon kneel, and the Deacon says the following prayer:

'Vouchsafe thine aid, Almighty Father of the universe, to this our present convention; and grant that this Candidate for Masonry may dedicate and devote his life to thy service, and become a true and faithful brother among us! Induce him with a competency of thy divine wisdom, that by the secrets of our art, he may be the better enabled to display the beauties of holiness to the honor of thy holy name. So mote it be. Amen!'

The Master then asks the Candidate, 'In whom do you put your trust?' *Ans.* 'In God.' The Master then takes him by the right-hand, and says, 'Since in God you put your trust, arise, follow your leader and fear no danger?' The Senior Deacon then conducts the Candidate three times regularly round the Lodge, and halts at the Junior Warden in the South, where the same questions are asked and answers returned as at the door.

As the Candidate and conductor are passing round the room the Master reads the following passage of Scripture, and takes the same time to read it that they do to go round the Lodge three times.

'Behold how good and how pleasant it is for Brethern to dwell together in unity! It is like the precious ointment upon the head, that ran down upon the beard, even Aaron's beard, that went down to the skirts of his garment: as the dew of Hermon, and as the dew that descended upon the mountains of Zion; for there the Lord commanded the blessing, even life forever more.'

The Candidate is then conducted to the Senior Warden in the West, where the same questions are asked and answers returned as before; from thence he is conducted to the Worshipful Master in the east, where the same questions are asked and answers returned as before. The Master likewise demands of him, from whence he came and whither he is traveling. The Candidate answers, 'From the West and traveling to the East.' Master inquires; 'Why do you leave the West and travel to the East?' *Ans.* 'In search of light.' Master then says, 'Since the Candidate is traveling in search of light, you will please conduct him back to the West, from whence he came, and put him in the care of the Senior Warden, who will teach him how to approach the East, the place of light, by advancing upon one upright regular step, to the first step, his feet forming the right angle of an oblong square, his body erect at the altar before the Master, and place him in a proper position to take upon him the solemn oath of obligation of an Entered Apprentice Mason.' The Senior Warden receives the Candidate, and instructs him as directed. He first steps off with the left foot and brings up the heel of the right into the hollow thereof, the heel of the right foot against the ankle of the left, will of course form the right angle of an oblong square; the Candidate then kneels on his left knee, and places his right foot so as to form a square with the left, he turns his foot round until the ankle bone is as much in front of him as the toes on the left foot; the Candidate's left hand is then put under the Holy Bible, square and compass, and the right on them. This is the position in which a Candidate is placed when he takes upon him the oath or obligation of an Entered Apprentice Mason. As soon as the Candidate is placed in this position, the Worshipful Master approaches him, and says, 'Mr. A. B., you are now placed in a proper position to take upon you the solemn oath or obligation of an Entered Apprentice Mason, which I assure you is neither to affect your religion nor politics, if you are willing to take it, repeat your name and say after me;' [and although many have refused to take any kind of an obligation, and begged for the privilege of retiring, yet none have made their escape; they have been either coerced, or persuaded to submit. There are thousands who never return to the Lodge after they are initiated] the following obligation is then administered:

'I, A. B., of my own free will and accord, in presence of Almighty God and this worshipful Lodge of free and accepted Masons, dedicated to God and held forth to the holy order of St. John, do hereby and herein most solemnly and sincerely promise and swear that I will always hail, ever conceal, and never reveal any part, or parts, art, or arts, point, or points of the secret arts and mysteries of ancient Freemasonry, which I have received, am about to receive, or may hereafter be instructed in, to any person, or persons in the known world, except it be to a true and lawful Brother Mason, or within the body of a just and lawfully constituted Lodge, of such; and not unto him, nor unto them whom I shall hear so to be, but unto him and them only whom I shall find so to be after strict trial and due examination or lawful information. Furthermore, do I promise and swear that I will not write, print, stamp, stain, hew, cut, carve, indent, paint, or engrave it on anything movable or immovable, under the whole canopy of Heaven, whereby, or whereon the least letter, figure, character, mark, stain, shadow, or resemblance of the same may become legible or intelligible to myself or any other person in the known world, whereby the secrets of Masonry may be unlawfully obtained through my unworthiness. To all which I do most solemnly and sincerely promise and swear, without the least equivocation, mental reservation, or self evasion of mind in me whatever; binding myself under no less penalty, than to have my throat cut across, my tongue torn out by the roots and my body buried in the rough sands of the sea at low water-mark, where the tide ebbs and flows twice in twenty-four hours; so help me God, and keep me steadfast in the due performance of the same.'

After the obligation the Master addresses the candidate in the following manner: 'Brother, to you the secrets of Masonry are about to be unvailed, and a brighter sun never shone luster on your eyes: while prostrate before this sacred altar, do you not shudder at every crime? have you not confidence in every virtue? May these thoughts ever inspire you with the most noble sentiments; may you ever feel that elevation of soul, that shall scorn a dishonest act. Brother, what do you most desire?' *Ans.* 'Light.' Master to Brethren, 'Brethren, stretch forth your hands and assist in bringing this new made Brother from darkness to light.' The members having formed a circle round the Candidate, the Master says, 'And God said, let there be light, and there was light.' At the same time, all the Brethren clap their hands, and stamp on the floor with their right foot as heavy as possible, the bandage dropping from the Candidate's eyes at the same instant, which, after having been so long blind, and full of fearful apprehension all the time, this great and sudden transition from perfect darkness to a light brighter (if possible) than the meridian sun in a midsummer day, sometimes produces an alarming effect. I once knew a man to faint on being brought to light; and his recovery was quite doubtful for some time: however, he did come to, but he never returned to the Lodge again. I have often conversed with him on the subject; he is yet living, and will give a certificate in support of the above statement at any time, if requested.

After the Candidate is brought to light, the Master addresses him as follows; 'Brother, on being brought to light, you first discover three great lights, in Masonry, by the assistance of three lesser; they are thus explained: the three great lights in Masonry are the Holy Bible, Square, and Compass. The Holy Bible is given to us as a rule and guide for our faith and practice; the Square, to square our actions; and the Compass, to keep us in due bounds with all mankind, but more especially with the Brethren. The three lesser lights are three burning tapers, or candles placed on candlesticks (some say or candles on pedestals), they represent the Sun, Moon and Master of the Lodge, and are thus explained. As the sun rules the day and the moon governs the night, so ought the Worshipful Master with equal regularity to rule and govern his Lodge, or cause the same to be done; you next discover me as Master of this Lodge, approaching you from the East upon the first step of Masonry, under the sign and due-guard of an Entered Apprentice Mason. (The sign and due-guard has been explained.) This is the manner of giving them; imitate me as near as you can, keeping your position. First, step off with your left foot and bring the heel of the right into the hollow thereof, so as to form a square.' (This is the first step in Masonry.) The following is the sign of an Entered Apprentice Mason, and is the sign of distress in this degree; you are not to give it unless in distress. (It is given by holding your two hands transversely across each other, the right-hand upward and one inch from the left.) The following is the due-guard of an Entered Apprentice Mason. (This is given by drawing your right-hand across your throat, the thumb next to your throat, your arm as high as the elbow in a horizontal position.) 'Brother, I now present you my right-hand in token of brotherly love and esteem, and with it the grip and name of the grip of an Entered Apprentice Mason.' The right-hands are joined together as in shaking hands, and each sticks his thumb nail nto the third joint or upper end of the fore-finger; the name of the grip is *Boaz*, and is to be given in the following manner and no other; the Master first gives the grip and word, and divides it for the instruction of the Candidate; the questions are as follows: The Master and Candidate holding each other by the grip, as before described, the Master says, 'What is this.' *Ans*. 'A grip.' *Q*. 'The grip of what.' *A*. 'The grip of an Entered Apprentice Mason.' *Q*. 'Has it a name?' *A*. 'It has.' *Q*. 'Will you give it to me?' *A*. 'I did not so receive it, neither can I so impart it.' *Q*. 'What will you do with it?' *A*. 'Letter it or halve it.' *Q*. 'Halve it and begin.' *A*. 'You begin.' *Q*. 'Begin you.' *A*. 'B O.' *Q*. 'A Z.' *A*. 'BOAZ.' Master says, 'Right, Brother *Boaz*, I greet you. It is the name of the left-hand pillar of the porch of king Solomon's Temple—arise, Brother Boaz, and salute the Junior and Senior Wardens as such, and convince them that you have been regularly initiated as an Entered Apprentice Mason, and have got the sign, grip, and word.' The Master returns to his seat while the wardens are examining the Candidate, and gets a lamb-skin or white apron, presents it to the Candidate, and observes, 'Brother, I now present you with a lamb-skin or white apron; it is an emblem of innocence, and the badge of a Mason: it has been worn by kings, princes, and potentates of the earth, who have never been ashamed to wear it; it is more honorable than the diadems of kings, or pearls of princesses, when worthily worn; it is more ancient than the Golden Fleece or Roman Eagle; more honorable than the Star and Garter, or any other order that can be conferred upon you at this, or any other time, except it be in the body of a just and lawfully constituted Lodge; you will carry it to the Senior Warden in the West, who will teach you how to wear it as an Entered Apprentice Mason.' The Senior Warden ties the apron on and turns up the flap instead of letting it fall down in front of the top of the apron. This is the way Entered Apprentice Masons wear, or ought to wear their aprons until they are advanced. The Candidate is now conducted to the Master in the East, who says, 'Brother, as you are dressed, it is necessary you should have tools to work with; I will now present you with the working tools of an Entered Apprentice Mason, which are the twenty-four inch gauge and common gavel: they are thus explained:—The twenty-four inch gauge is an instrument made use of by operative Masons to measure and lay out their work, but we, as Free and Accepted Masons, make use of it for the more noble and glorious purpose of dividing our time. The twenty-four inches on the gauge, are emblematical of the twenty-four hours in the day, which we are taught to divide into three equal parts, whereby we find eight hours for the service of God, and a worthy distressed brother; eight hours for our usual vocations, and eight for refreshment and sleep; the common gavel is an instrument made use of by operative Masons to break off the corners of rough stones; the better to fit them for the builders' use, but we, as Free and Accepted Masons use it for the more noble and glorious purpose of

B

divesting our hearts and consciences of all the vices and superfluities of life, thereby fitting our minds as living and lively stones, for that spiritual building, that house not made with hands, eternal in the heavens; I also present you with a new name; it is CAUTION, it teaches you that as you are barely instructed in the rudiments of Masonry, that you should be cautious over all your words and actions, particularly when before the enemies of Masonry. I shall next present you with three precious jewels, which are; a *listening ear*, a *silent tongue*, and a *faithful heart*. A listening ear teaches you to listen to the instructions of the Worshipful Master; but more especially that you should listen to the calls and cries of a worthy distressed brother. A silent tongue teaches you to be silent while in the Lodge, that the peace and harmony thereof may not be disturbed, but more especially, that you should be silent before the enemies of Masonry, that the craft may not be brought into disrepute by your imprudence. A faithful heart teaches you to be faithful to the instructions of the Worshipful Master at all times, but more especially, that you should be faithful, and keep and conceal the secrets of Masonry, and those of a Brother when given to you in charge as such, that they may remain as secure and inviolable in your breast as in his own, before communicated to you. I further present you with check-words two; their names are *truth* and *union*, and are thus explained. Truth is a divine attribute, and the foundation of every virtue; to be good and true, is the first lesson we are taught in Masonry; on this theme we contemplate, and by its dictates endeavor to regulate our conduct hence, while influenced by this principle hypocrisy and deceit are unknown among us; sincerity and plain dealing distinguish us, and the heart and tongue join in promoting each other's welfare and rejoicing in each other's prosperity.

Union, is that kind of friendship, which ought to appear conspicuous in every Mason's conduct. It is so closely allied to the Divine attribute, truth, that he who enjoys the one, is seldom destitute of the other. Should interest, honor, prejudice, or human depravity, ever induce you to violate any part of the sacred trust we now repose in you, let these two important words, at the earliest insinuation, teach you to put on the check-line of truth, which will infallibly direct you to pursue that straight and narrow path which ends in the full enjoyment of the Grand Lodge above; where we shall all meet as Masons and members of the same family, in peace, harmony and love; where all discord on account of politics, religion, or private opinion shall be unknown, and banished from within our walls.

Brother, it has been the custom from time immemorial to demand, or ask from a newly made Brother something of a metallic kind, not so much on account of its intrinsic value, but that it may be deposited in the archives of the Lodge, as a memorial, that you was herein made a Mason;—a small trifle will be sufficient;—anything of a metallic kind will do; if you have no money, anything of a metallic nature will be sufficient; even a button will do.' (The candidate says he has nothing about him; it is known he has nothing.) 'Search yourself,' the Master replies. He is assisted in searching, nothing is found; 'perhaps you can borrow a trifle,' says the Master. (He tries to borrow, none will lend him—he proposes to go into the other room where his clothes are; he is not permitted.—If a stranger, he is very much embarrassed. Master to candidate, 'Brother, let this ever be a striking lesson to you, and teach you, if you should ever see a friend, but more especially a brother in a like pennyless situation, to contribute as liberally to his relief as his situation may require, and your abilities will admit, without material injury to yourself or family.' Master to Senior Deacon, 'You will conduct the candidate back from whence he came, and invest him of what he has been divested, and let him return for further instruction.' The candidate is then conducted to the preparation room, and invested of what he had been divested, and returns to the North-East corner of the Lodge, and is taught how to stand upright like a man; when and where the following charge is, or ought to be delivered to him; though it is omitted nine times out of ten, as are near one-half of the ceremonies.

Master to the Candidate, 'Brother, as you are now initiated into the first principles of Masonry, I congratulate you upon having been accepted into this ancient and honorable order; ancient, as having subsisted from time immemorial; and honorable, as tending in every particular so to render all men who will be conformable to its principles. No institution was ever raised on a better principle, or more solid foundation, nor were ever more excellent rules and useful maxims laid down than are inculcated in the several masonic lectures. The greatest and best of men in all ages have been encouragers and promoters of the art, and have never deemed it derogatory to their dignity, to level themselves with the fraternity—extend their privileges, and patronize their assemblies.'

'There are three great duties, which, as a Mason, you are charged to inculcate. To God, your neighbor, and yourself. To God, in never mentioning his name, but with that reverential awe that is due from a creature to his Creator; to implore his aid in all your laudable undertakings, and to esteem him as the chief Good—To your neighbor, in acting upon the square, and doing unto him as you wish he should do unto you; and to yourself in avoiding all irregularity or intemperance, which may impair your faculties, or debase the dignity of your profession. A zealous attachment to these principles will ensure public and private esteem. In the state, you are to be a quiet and peaceable subject, true to your government and just to your country; you are not to countenance disloyalty, but faithfully to submit to legal authority, and conform with cheerfulness to the government of the country in which you live. In your outward demeanor be particularly careful to avoid censure or reproach. Although your frequent appearance at our regular meetings is earnestly solicited, yet it is not meant that Masonry should interfere with your necessary vocations; for these are on no account to be neglected: neither are you to suffer your zeal for the institution to lead you into argument with those, who, through ignorance, may ridicule it. At your leisure hours, that you may improve in masonic knowledge, you are to converse with well-informed Brethren, who will be always as ready to give, as you will be to receive information. Finally, keep sacred and inviolable the mysteries of the order, as these are to distinguish you from the rest of the community, and mark your consequence among Masons. If, in the circle of your acquaintance, you find a person desirous of being initiated into Masonry, be particularly attentive not to recommend him, unless you are convinced he will conform to our rules; that the honor, glory, and reputation of the institution may be firmly established, and the world at large convinced of its good effects.

The work of the evening being over, I will proceed to give a description of the manner of closing the Lodge. It is a very common practice, in Lodges, to close a Lodge of Entered Apprentices, and open a Lodge of Fellow Crafts, and close that, and open a Master Masons' Lodge, all in the same evening.

Some Brother generally makes a motion that the Lodge be closed; it being seconded and carried:—

The Master to the Junior Deacon—'Brother Junior,' (giving one rap which calls up both Deacons), 'The first as well as the last care of a Mason?' *Ans.* 'To see the Lodge tyled, Worshipful.' Master to Junior Deacon, 'Attend to that part of your duty, and inform the Tyler, that we are about to close this Lodge of Entered Apprentice Masons, and direct him to tyle accordingly.' The Junior Deacon steps to the door, and gives three raps, which are answered by the Tyler with three more; the Junior Deacon then gives one, which is also answered by the Tyler by one. The Junior Deacon then opens the door, delivers his message, and resumes his place in the Lodge, and says, 'The door is tyled, Worshipful.' Master to Junior Deacon, 'By whom?' *Ans.* 'By a Master Mason without the door, armed with the proper implement of his office.' Master to Junior Deacon, 'His business there?' *Ans.* 'To keep of all cowans and eaves-droppers, and see that none pass or repass without permission from the chair.' Master to Junior Deacon, 'Your place in the Lodge, Brother Junior?' *Ans.* 'At the right-hand of the Senior Warden in the West.' Master to Junior Deacon, 'Your duty there?' *Ans.* 'To wait on the Worshipful Master and Wardens, act as their proxy in the active duties of the Lodge, and take charge of the door.' Master to the Junior Deacon, 'The Senior Deacon's place in the Lodge?' *Ans.* 'At the right-hand of the Worshipful Master in the East.' Master to Senior Deacon, 'Your duty there, Brother Senior?' *Ans.* 'To wait on the Worshipful Master and Wardens, act as their proxy in the active duties of the Lodge; attend to the preparation and introduction of Candidates, receive and clothe all visiting Brethren.' Master to the Senior Deacon, 'The Secretary's place in the Lodge?' *Ans.* 'At your left-hand, Worshipful.' Master to Secretary, 'Your duty there, Brother Secretary?' *Ans.* 'Duly to observe the Master's will and pleasure; record the proceedings of the Lodge; transmit a copy of the same to the Grand Lodge, if required; receive all moneys and money bills from the hands of the Brethren; pay them over to the Treasurer, and take his receipt for the same.' Master to the Secretary, 'The Treasurer's place in the Lodge?' *Ans.* 'At the right-hand of the Worshipful Master.' Master to Treasurer, 'Your business there, Brother Treasurer?' *Ans.* 'Duly to observe the Worshipful Master's will and pleasure; receive all moneys and money bills from the hands of the Secretary; keep a just and accurate account of the same; pay them out by order of the Worshipful Master and consent of the Brethren.' Master to the Treasurer, 'The Junior Warden's place in the Lodge?' *Ans.* 'In the South, Worshipful.' Master to the Junior Warden, 'Your business there, Brother Junior?' *Ans.* 'As the sun in the South, at high meridian, is the beauty and glory of the day; so stands the Junior Warden in the South, at high twelve, the better to observe the time; call the Crafts from labor to refreshment; superintend them during the hours thereof; see that none convert the purposes of refreshment into that of excess or intemperance; call them on again in due season, that the Worshipful Master may have honor, and they pleasure and profit thereby.' The Master, to the Junior Warden [I wish the reader to take particular notice, that in closing the Lodge, the Master asks the Junior Warden as follows: 'The Master's place in the Lodge?' and in opening he asks the Senior Warden the same question] 'The Master's place in the Lodge?' *Ans.* 'In the East, Worshipful.' Master to Junior Warden, 'His duty there?' *Ans.* 'As the sun rises in the East, to open and adorn the day, so presides the Worshipful Master in the East, to open and adorn his Lodge; set his crafts to work with good and wholesome laws, or cause the same to be done.' Master to the Junior Warden, 'The Senior Warden's place in the Lodge?' *Ans.* 'In the West, Worshipful.' Master to Senior Warden, 'Your business there, Brother Senior?' *Ans.* 'As the sun sets in the West to close the day, so stands the Senior Warden in the West, to assist the Worshipful Master in opening and closing the Lodge; take care of the jewels and implements; see that none be lost; pay the crafts their wages, if any be due, and see that none go away dissatisfied.' The Master now gives three raps, when all the Brethren rise, and the Master asks, 'Are you all satisfied?' They answer in the affirmative, by giving the due-guard. Should the Master discover that any declined giving it, inquiry is immediately made, why it is so; and if any member is dissatisfied with any part of the proceedings, or with any Brother, the subject is immediately investigated. Master to the Brethren,

'Attend to giving the signs; as I do, so do you; give them downwards, (which is by giving the last in opening, first in closing. In closing, on this degree, you first draw your right-hand across your throat, as hereinbefore described, and then hold your two hands over each other, as before described This is the method pursued through all the degrees; and when opening on any of the upper degrees, all the signs of all the preceding degrees, are given before you give the signs of the degree, on which you are opening.) This being done, the Master proceeds, 'I now declare this Lodge of Entered Apprentice Masons, regularly closed in due and ancient form. Brother Junior Warden, please inform Brother Senior Warden, and request him to inform the Brethren, that it is my will and pleasure, that this Lodge of Entered Apprentice Masons be now closed, and stand closed until our next regular communication, unless a case or cases of emergency, shall require earlier convention, of which every member shall be notified; during which time, it is seriously hoped, and expected, that every Brother will demean himself as becomes a Free and Accepted Mason.' Junior Warden to Senior Warden, 'Brother Senior, it is the Worshipful Master's will and pleasure, that this Lodge of Entered Apprentice Masons be closed, and stand closed until our next regular communication, unless a case or cases of emergency shall require earlier convention, of which every Brother shall be notified; during which time it is seriously hoped, and expected, that every Brother will demean himself as becomes a Free and Accepted Mason.' Senior Warden to the Brethren, 'Brethren, you have heard the Worshipful Master's will and pleasure, as communicated to me by Brother Junior; so let it be done.' Master to the Junior Warden, 'Brother Junior, how do Masons meet?' *Ans.* 'On the level.' Master to Senior Warden, 'How do Masons part?' *Ans.* 'On the square.' Master to the Junior and Senior Wardens, 'Since we meet on the level, Brother Junior, and part on the square, Brother Senior, so let us ever meet and part, in the name of the Lord.' Here follows a prayer, sometimes used. Master to the Brethren, 'Brethren, let us pray.'

'Supreme Architect of the Universe! accept our humble praises for the many mercies and blessings which thy bounty has conferred upon us, and especially for this friendly and social intercourse. Pardon, we beseech thee, whatever thou hast seen amiss in us since we have been together; and continue to us thy presence, protection, and blessing. Make us sensible of the renewed obligations we are under to love thee supremely, and to be friendly to each other. May all our irregular passions be subdued, and may we daily increase in faith, hope and charity, but more especially in that charity, which is the bond of peace, and perfection of every virtue. May we so practice thy precepts, that through the merits of the Redeemer, we may finally obtain thy promises, and find an acceptance through the gates, and into the Temple and City of our God. So mote it be. Amen.'

A BENEDICTION OFTENER USED AT CLOSING THAN THE PRECEDING PRAYER.

May the blessing of Heaven rest upon us and all regular Masons; may brotherly love prevail, and every moral and social virtue cement us. So mote it be. Amen.

After the prayer the following charge ought to be delivered; but it is seldom attended to; in a majority of Lodges it is never attended to.

Master to Brethren, 'Brethren, we are now about to quit this sacred retreat of friendship and virtue, to mix again with the world. Amidst its concerns and employments forget not the duties which you have heard so frequently inculcated, and so forcibly recommended in this Lodge. Remember that around this altar, you have promised to befriend and relieve every Brother who shall need your assistance. You have promised in the most friendly manner to remind him of his errors, and aid in reformation. These generous principles are to extend further: every human being has a claim upon your kind offices. Do good unto all. Recommend it more 'especially to the household of the faithful.' Finally, Brethren, be ye all of one mind, live in peace, and may the God of love and peace, delight to dwell with and bless you.

In some Lodges, after the charge is delivered, the Master says, 'Brethren, form on the square.' When all the Brethren form a circle, and the Master followed by every Brother (except in using the words) says, 'And God said, let there be light, and there was light.' At the same moment that the last of these words drop from the Master's lips, every member stamps with his right-foot on the floor, and at the same instant, bring their hands together with equal force, and in such perfect unison with each other, that persons situated so as to hear it, would suppose it the precursor of some dreadful catastrophe. This is called *the shock.*'

Having described all the ceremonies and forms appertaining to the opening of a Lodge of Entered Apprentice Masons; setting them to work; initiating a Candidate, and closing the Lodge, I will now proceed to give the Lecture on this degree. It is divided into three sections. The lecture is nothing more or less than a recapitulation of the preceding ceremonies and forms by way of question and answer, and fully explains the same. In fact, the ceremonies and forms (generally Masonically called *the work*), and lectures are so much the same, that he who possesses a knowledge of the lectures, cannot be destitute of a knowledge of what the ceremonies and forms are. As the ceremonies used in opening and closing are the same in all the degrees, it is thought best to give the whole one insertion; it being the sincere wish of the writer, that every reader should perfectly understand all the formulas of the whole Masonic fabric, as he then will thereby be able to form correct opinions of the propriety or impropriety, advantages or disadvantages of the same.

FIRST SECTION OF THE LECTURE ON THE FIRST DEGREE OF MASONRY.

Q. From whence come you as an Entered Apprentice Mason?
A. From the holy Lodge of St. John, at Jerusalem.
Q. What recommendations do you bring?
A. Recommendations from the Worshipful Master, Wardens and Brethren of that Right Worshipful Lodge, whom greet you.
Q. What comest thou hither to do?
A. To learn to subdue my passions, and improve myself in the secret arts and mysteries of ancient Free Masonry.
Q. You are a Mason then, I presume?
A. I am.
Q. How shall I know you to be a Mason?
A. By certain signs and a token.
Q. What are signs?
A. All right angles, horizontals, and perpendiculars.
Q. What is a token?
A. A certain, friendly and brotherly grip, whereby one Mason may know another in the dark as well as in the light.
Q. Where was you first proposed to be made a Mason?
A. In my heart.
Q. Where secondly?
A. In a room adjacent to the body of a just and lawfully constituted Lodge of such.
Q. How was you prepared?
A. By being divested of all metals, neither naked nor clothed, barefoot nor shod, hoodwinked, with a Cable-Tow* about my neck, in which situation I was conducted to the door of the Lodge.
Q. You being hoodwinked, how did you know it to be a door?
A. By first meeting with resistance and afterward gaining admission.
Q. How did you gain admission?
A. By three distinct knocks from without, answered by the same from within.
Q. What was said to you from within?
A. Who comes there, who comes there, who comes there.

---
* Three miles long.

Q. Your answer?

A. A poor blind Candidate who has long been desirous of having and receiving a part of the rights and benefits of this Worshipful Lodge, dedicated to God, and held forth to the holy order of St. John, as all true fellows and brothers have done, who have gone this way before me.

Q. What further was said to you from within?

A. I was asked if it was of my own free will and accord I made this request, if I was duly and truly proposed, worthy and well qualified; all of which being answered in the affirmative, I was asked by what further rights I expected to obtain so great a favor or benefit.

Q. Your answer?

A. By being a man, free born, of lawful age and well recommended.

Q. What was then said to you?

A. I was bid to wait until the Worshipful Master in the East was made acquainted with my request and his answer returned.

Q. After his answer returned what followed?

A. I was caused to enter the Lodge.

Q. How?

A. On the point of some sharp instrument pressing my naked left breast In the name of the Lord.

Q. How was you then disposed of?

A. I was conducted to the center of the Lodge and there caused to kneel for the benefit of a prayer. [See page 18.]

Q. After prayer what was said to you?

A. I was asked in whom I put my trust.

Q. Your answer?

A. In God.

Q. What followed?

A. The Worshipful Master took me by the right-hand and said, since In God you trust, arise, follow your leader and fear no danger.

Q. How was you then disposed of?

A. I was conducted three times regularly round the Lodge and halted at the Junior Warden in the South, where the same questions were asked and answers returned as at the door.

Q. How did the Junior Warden dispose of you?

A. He ordered me to be conducted to the Senior Warden in the West, where the same questions were asked and answers returned as before.

Q. How did the Senior Warden dispose of you?

A. He ordered me to be conducted to the Worshipful Master in the East, where the same questions were asked and answers returned as before, who likewise demanded of me from whence I came and whither I was traveling.

Q. Your answer?

A. From the West and traveling to the East.

Q. Why do you leave the West and travel to the East?
A. In search of light.
Q. How did the Worshipful Master then dispose of you?
A. He ordered me to be conducted back to the West, from whence I came, and put in care of the Senior Warden, who taught me how to approach the East, the place of light, by advancing upon one upright regular step to the first step, my feet forming the right angle of an oblong square, my body erect at the altar before the Worshipful Master.
Q. What did the Worshipful Master do with you?
A. He made an Entered Apprentice Mason of me.
Q. How?
A. In due form.
Q. What was that due form?
A My left knee bare bent, my right forming a square; my left hand supporting the Holy Bible, Square, and Compass, and my right covering the same; in which position I took upon me the solemn oath or obligation of an Entered Apprentice Mason. (See page 19.)
Q. After you had taken your obligation what was said to you?
A. I was asked what I most desired.
Q. Your answer?
A. Light.
Q. Was you immediately brought to light?
A. I was.
Q. How?
A. By the direction of the Master and assistance of the Brethren.
Q. What did you first discover after being brought to light?
A. Three great Lights, in Masonry, by the assistance of three lesser.
Q. What were those three great Lights in Masonry?
A. The Holy Bible, Square, and Compass.
Q. How are they explained?
A. The Holy Bible is given to us as a guide for our faith and practice, the Square, to square our actions; and the Compass, to keep us in due bounds with all mankind, but more especially with the Brethren.
Q. What were those three lesser lights?
A. Three burning tapers, or candles on candlesticks.
Q. What do they represent?
A. The Sun, Moon, and Master of the Lodge.
Q. How are they explained?
A. As the Sun rules the day and the Moon governs the night, so ought the Worshipful Master to use his endeavors to rule and govern his Lodge with equal regularity, or cause the same to be done.
Q. What did you next discover?
A. The Worshipful Master approaching me from the East, under the sign

and due-guard of an Entered Apprentice Mason, who presented me with his right-hand in token of brotherly love and esteem, and proceeded to give me the grip and word of an Entered Apprentice Mason, and bid me rise and salute the Junior and Senior Wardens and convince them that I had been regularly initiated as an Entered Apprentice Mason, and was in possession of the sign, grip and word.

Q. What did you next discover?

A. The Worshipful Master a second time approaching me from the East, who presented me with a lamb-skin or white apron, which he said was an emblem of innocence, and the badge of a Mason; that it had been worn by kings, princes and potentates of the earth who had never been ashamed to wear it; that it was more honorable than the diadems of kings, or pearls of princesses, when worthily worn, and more ancient than the Golden Fleece or Roman Eagle, more honorable than the star or garter, or any other order that could be conferred upon me at that time or any time thereafter, except it be in the body of a just and lawfully constituted Lodge of Masons; and bid me carry it to the Senior Warden in the West, who taught me how to wear it as an Entered Apprentice Mason.

Q. What was you next presented with?

A. The working tools of an Entered Apprentice Mason.

Q. What were they?

A. The twenty-four inch gauge and common gavel.

Q. How are they explained?

A. The twenty-four inch gauge is an instrument made use of by operative Masons to measure and lay out their work, but we, as Free and Accepted Masons are taught to make use of it for the more noble and glorious purpose of dividing our time; the twenty-four inches on the gauge are emblematical of the twenty-four hours in the day, which we are taught to divide into three equal parts, whereby we find eight hours for the service of God and a worthy distressed Brother, eight hours for our usual vocation, and eight hours for refreshment and sleep.—The common gavel is an instrument made use of by operative Masons to break off the corners of rough stones, the better to fit them for the builders' use, but we, as Free and Accepted Masons, are taught to make use of it for the more noble and glorious purpose of divesting our hearts and consciences of all the vices and superfluities of life, thereby fitting our minds as lively and living stones for that spiritual building, that house not made with hands, eternal in the heavens.

Q. What was you next presented with?

A. A new name.

Q. What was that?

A. Caution.

Q. What does it teach?

A. It teaches me as I was barely instructed in the rudiments of Masonry, that I should be cautious over all my words and actions, especially when before its enemies.

Q. What was you next presented with?
A. Three precious jewels.
Q. What were they?
A. A listening ear, a silent tongue, and a faithful heart.
Q. What do they teach?
A. A listening ear, teaches me to listen to the instruction of the Worshipful Master, but more especially, that I should listen to the calls and cries of a worthy distressed Brother. A silent tongue, teaches me to be silent in the Lodge, that the peace and harmony thereof may not be disturbed; but more especially, that I should be silent when before the enemies of Masonry. A faithful heart, that I should be faithful to the instructions of the Worshipful Master, at all times, but more especially, that I should be faithful, and keep and conceal the secrets of Masonry, and those of a Brother, when delivered to me in charge, as such, that they may remain as secure and inviolable in my breast, as in his own, before communicated to me.

Q. What was you next presented with?
A. Check words two.
Q. What were they?
A. Truth and Union.
Q. How explained?
A. Truth, is a divine attribute, and the foundation of every virtue. To be good and true, are the first lessons we are taught in Masonry. On this theme we contemplate, and by its dictates endeavor to regulate our conduct; hence, while influenced by this principle, hypocrisy and deceit are unknown amongst us; sincerity and plain dealing distinguishes us; and the heart and tongue join in promoting each other's welfare, and rejoicing in each other's prosperity.

Union is that kind of friendship, that ought to appear conspicuous in the conduct of every Mason. It is so closely allied to the divine attribute truth, that he who enjoys the one, is seldom destitute of the other.—Should interest, honor, prejudice, or human depravity, ever influence you to violate any part of the sacred trust we now repose in you, let these two important words at the earliest insinuation, teach you to put on the check-line of truth, which will infallibly direct you to pursue that straight and narrow path, which ends in the full enjoyment of the Grand Lodge above, where we shall all meet, as Masons and members of one family; where all discord on account of religion, politics, or private opinion, will be unknown, and banished from within our walls.

Q. What followed?
A. The Worshipful Master in the East, made a demand of me, of something of a metallic kind, which he said was not so much on account of its

intrinsic value, as that it might be deposited in the archives of the Lodge, as a memorial that I had therein been made a Mason.

Q. How did the Worshipful Master then dispose of you?

A: He ordered me to be conducted out of the Lodge, and invested of what I had been divested, and returned for further instructions.

Q. After you returned, how was you disposed of?

A. I was conducted to the North-East corner of the Lodge, and there caused to stand upright like a man, my feet forming a square, and received a solemn injunction, ever to walk and act uprightly before God and man and in addition thereto received the following charge. (For this charge see page 27.)

SECOND SECTION.

Q. Why was you divested of all metals when you was made a Mason?

A. Because Masonry regards no man on account of his worldly wealth or honors; it is therefore the internal, and not the external qualifications that recommend a man to Masons.

Q. A second reason?

A. There was neither the sound of an ax, hammer, or any other metal tool, heard at the building of King Solomon's Temple.

Q. How could so stupendous a fabric be erected without the sound of an ax, hammer, or any other metal tool?

A. All the stones were hewed, squared, and numbered in the quarries, where they were raised; all the timbers felled, and prepared in the forests of Lebanon, and carried down to Joppa on floats, and taken from thence up to Jerusalem, and set up with wooden malls, prepared for that purpose; which, when completed, every part thereof, fitted with that exact nicety, that it had more the resemblance of the handy workmanship of the Supreme Architect of the Universe, than that of human hands.

Q. Why was you neither naked nor clothed?

A. As I was an object of distress at that time, it was to remind me, if ever I saw a friend, more especially a Brother in a like distressed situation, that I should contribute as liberally to his relief, as his situation required, and my abilities would admit, without material injury to myself or family.

Q. Why was you neither barefoot nor shod?

A. It was an ancient Israelitish custom, adopted among Masons; and we read in the book of Ruth concerning their mode and manner of changing and redeeming, "and to confirm all things, a brother plucked off his shoe and gave it to his neighbor, and that was testimony in Israel." This, then, therefore we do in confirmation of a token, and as a pledge of our fidelity; thereby signifying that we will renounce our own wills in all things, and become obedient to the laws of our ancient institutions.

Q. Why was you hoodwinked?

A. That my heart might conceive, before my eyes beheld the beauties of Masonry.

Q. A second reason?

A. As I was in darkness at that time, it was to remind me that I should keep the whole world so respecting Masonry.

Q. Why had you a Cable-Tow about your neck?

A. In case I had not submitted to the manner and mode of my initiation that I might have been led out of the Lodge without seeing the form and beauties thereof.

Q. Why did you give three distinct knocks at the door?

A. To alarm the Lodge, and let the Worshipful Master, Wardens and Brethren know that a poor blind Candidate prayed admission.

Q. What do those three distinct knocks allude to?

A. A certain passage in Scripture, wherein it says, 'Ask and it shall be given, seek and ye shall find, knock and it shall be opened unto you.'

Q. How did you apply this to your then case in Masonry?

A. I asked the recommendations of a friend to become a Mason, I sought admission through his recommendations, and knocked and the door of Masonry opened unto me.

Q. Why was you caused to enter on the point of some sharp instrument pressing your naked left breast in the name of the Lord?

A. As this was a torture to my flesh, so might the recollection of it ever be to my heart and conscience, if ever I attempted to reveal the secrets of Masonry unlawfully.

Q. Why was you conducted to the center of the Lodge, and there caused to kneel for the benefit of a prayer?

A. Before entering on this, or any other great and important undertaking it is highly necessary to implore a blessing from Deity.

Q. Why was you asked in whom you put your trust?

A. Agreeably to the laws of our ancient institution, no Atheist could be made a Mason; it was therefore necessary that I should believe in Deity; otherwise, no oath or obligation could bind me.

Q. Why did the Worshipful Master take you by the right hand, and bid you rise, follow your leader and fear no danger?

A. As I was in darkness at that time and could neither foresee nor avoid danger, it was to remind me that I was in the hands of an affectionate friend in whose fidelity I might with safety confide.

Q. Why was you conducted three times regularly round the Lodge?

A. That the Worshipful Master, Wardens, and Brethren might see that I was duly and truly prepared.

Q. Why did you meet with those several obstructions on the way?

A. This and every other Lodge is, or ought to be, a true representation of King Solomon's Temple, which, when completed, had guards stationed at the East, West, and South gates.

Q. Why had they guards stationed at those several gates?

A. To prevent any one from passing or repassing that was not duly qualified.

Q. Why did you kneel on your left knee, and not on your right, or both?

A. The left side has ever been considered the weakest part of the body it was therefore to remind me that the part I was then taking upon me was the weakest part of Masonry, it being that only of an Entered Apprentice.

Q. Why was your right-hand placed on the Holy Bible, Square and Compass, and not your left, or both?

A. The right-hand has ever been considered the seat of fidelity, and our ancient Brethren, worshiped Deity under the name of FIDES; which has sometimes been represented by two right-hands joined together; at others, by two human figures holding each other by the right-hand; the right-hand, therefore, we use in this great and important undertaking, to signify in the strongest manner possible, the sincerity of our intentions in the business we are engaged.

Q. Why did the Worshipful Master present you with a lamb-skin, or white apron?

A. The lamb-skin has, in all ages, been deemed an emblem of innocence; he, therefore, who wears the lamb-skin, as a badge of a Mason, is thereby continually reminded of that purity of life, and rectitude of conduct, which is so essentially necessary to our gaining admission into the Celestial Lodge above, where the Supreme Architect of the Universe presides.

Q. Why did the Master make a demand of you of something of a metallic nature?

A. As I was in a poor and penniless situation at that time, it was to remind me if ever I saw a friend, but more especially, a Brother, in the like poor and penniless situation, that I should contribute as liberally to his relief as my abilities would admit and his situation required, without injuring myself or family.

Q. Why was you conducted to the north-east corner of the Lodge, and there caused to stand upright like a man, your feet forming a square, receiving at the same time a solemn charge, ever to walk and act uprightly before God and man?

A. The first stone in every Masonic edifice is, or ought to be, placed at the north-east corner, that being the place where an Entered Apprentice Mason receives his first instructions to build his future Masonic edifice upon.

THIRD SECTION.

Q. We have been saying a good deal about a Lodge, I want to know what constitutes a Lodge?

A. A certain number of Free and Accepted Masons duly assembled in a room, or place, with the Holy Bible, Square and Compass, and other Masonic implements, with a Charter from the Grand Lodge empowering them to work.

Q. Where did our ancient Brethren meet before Lodges were erected?

A. On the highest hills, and in the lowest vales.

Q. Why on the highest hills, and in the lowest vales?

A. The better to guard against cowans and enemies either ascending or descending, that the Brethren might have timely notice of their approach to prevent being surprised.

Q. What is the form of your Lodge?

A. An oblong square.

Q. How long? A. From East to West.

Q. How wide? A. Between North and South.

Q. How high? A. From the surface of the earth to the highest heavens.

Q. How deep? A. From the surface to the center.

Q. What supports your Lodge?

A. Three large Columns or Pillars.

Q. What are their names?

A. Wisdom, Strength, and Beauty.

Q. Why so? A. It is necessary there should be Wisdom to contrive, Strength to support, and Beauty to adorn all great and important undertakings; but more especially this of ours.

Q. Has your Lodge any covering?

A. It has a clouded canopy, or starry-decked heaven, where all good Mason's hope to arrive.

Q. How do they hope to arrive there?

A. By the assistance of Jacob's ladder.

Q. How many principal rounds has it got?

A. Three. Q. What are their names?

A. Faith, Hope, and Charity.

Q. What do they teach?

A. Faith in God, Hope in immortality, and Charity to all mankind.

Q. Has your Lodge any furniture?

A. It has, the Holy Bible, Square, and Compass.

Q. To whom do they belong?

A. The Bible to God, the Square to the Master, and the Compass to the Craft.

Q. How explained?

A. The Bible to God, in being the inestimable gift of God to man, for his instruction to guide him through the rugged paths of life; the Square to the Master, it being the proper emblem of his office; the Compass to the Craft—by due attention to which, we are taught to limit our desires, curb our ambition, subdue our irregular appetites, and keep our passions and prejudices in due bounds with all mankind, but more especially with the Brethren.

Q. Has your Lodge any ornaments?

A. It has; the Mosaic, or chequered pavement; the indented Tessel, that beautiful tesselated border which surrounds it, with the blazing star in the center.

Q. What do they represent?

A. The Mosaic, or chequered pavement, represents this world, which, though chequered over with good and evil, yet Brethren may walk together thereon and not stumble—the indented Tessel, with the blazing star in the center, the manifold blessings and comforts with which we are surrounded in this life, but more especially those which we hope to enjoy hereafter — the Blazing star, the prudence which ought to appear conspicuous in the conduct of every Mason; but more especially commemorative of the Star which appeared in the East, to guide the wise men to Bethlehem, to proclaim the birth and the presence of the Son of God,

Q. Has your Lodge any lights?

A. It has three.

Q. How are they situated?

A. East, West and South.

Q. Has it none in the North?

A. It has not.

Q. Why so?

A. Because this and every other Lodge is, or ought to be, a true representation of King Solomon's Temple, which was situated north of the ecliptic; the sun and moon therefore during their rays from the south, no light was to be expected from the north; we, therefore, Masonically, term the north a place of darkness.

Q. Has your Lodge any Jewels?

A. It has six; three movable and three immovable.

Q. What are the three movable Jewels?

A. The Square, Level and Plumb.

Q. What do they teach?

A. The Square, morality; the Level, equality; and the Plumb, rectitude of life and conduct.

Q. What are the three movable Jewels?

A. The rough Ashlar, the perfect Ashlar, and the Trestle-Board.

C

Q. What are they?

A. The rough Ashlar, is a stone in its rough and natural state; the perfect Ashlar is also a stone made ready by the working tools of the Fellow-Craft to be adjusted in the building; and the Trestle-board is for the Master workman to draw his plans and designs upon.

Q. What do they represent?

A. The rough Ashlar represents man in his rude and imperfect state by nature; the perfect Ashlar also represents man in that state of perfection to which we all hope to arrive by means of a virtuous life and education, our own endeavors, and the blessing of God. In erecting our temporal building we pursue the plans and designs laid down by the master workman on his Trestle-board; but in erecting our spiritual building we pursue the plans and designs laid down by the Supreme Geometrician of the Universe in the Book of life which we, Masonically, term our spiritual trestle-board.

Q. Whom did you serve?

A. My Master

Q. How long?

A. Six days.

Q. What did you serve him with

A. Freedom, fervency and zeal.

Q. What do they represent?

A. Chalk, Charcoal, and Earth.

Q. Why so?

A. There is nothing freer than Chalk, the slightest touch of which leaves a trace behind; nothing more fervent than heated Charcoal; it will melt the most obdurate metals; nothing more zealous than the Earth to bring forth.

Q. How is your Lodge situated?

A. Due east and west.

Q. Why so?

A. Because the sun rises in the east and sets in the west.

Q. A second reason?

A. The Gospel was first preached in the east, and is spreading to the west.

Q. A third reason?

A. The liberal arts and sciences began in the east, and are extending to the west.

Q. A fourth reason?

A. Because all Churches and Chapels are, or ought to be, so situated.

Q. Why are all Churches and Chapels so situated?

A. Because King Solomon's Temple was so situated.

Q. Why was King Solomon's Temple so situated?

A. Because Moses, after conducting the Children of Israel through the

Red Sea, by Divine command, erected a tabernacle to God, and placed it due east and west; which was to comemmorate, to the latest posterity, that miraculous East wind that wrought their mighty deliverance; and this was an exact model of King Solomon's Temple. Since which time, every well-regulated and governed Lodge is, or ought to be, so situated.

Q. To whom did our ancient Brethren dedicate their Lodges?

A. To King Solomon.

Q. Why so? A. Because King Solomon was our most ancient Grand Master.

Q. To whom do modern Masons dedicate their Lodges?

A. To St. John the Baptist, and St. John the Evangelist.

Q. Why so? A. Because they were the two most ancient Christian patrons of Masonry: and since their time, in every well-regulated and governed Lodge, there has been a certain point within a circle, which circle is bounded on the East and the West by two perpendicular parallel lines, representing the anniversary of St. John the Baptist, and St. John the Evangelist, who were two perfect parallels as well in Masonry as Christianity; on the vortex of which rests the book of the Holy Scriptures, supporting Jacob's Ladder, which is said to reach to the watery clouds; and in passing round this circle we naturally touch on both these perpendicular parallel lines, as well as the Book of the Holy Scriptures, and while a Mason keeps himself thus circumscribed, he cannot materially err. [Thus ends the first degree of Masonry, and the reader, who has read and paid attention to it, knows more of Masonry, than any Entered Apprentice in Christendom, and more of this degree than one hundreth part of the Master Masons, or even Royal Arch Masons; for very few even attempt to learn the Lectures, or even the Obligations: They merely receive the degrees, and there stop, with the exception of a few who are fascinated with the idea of holding an office: they sometimes endeavor to qualify themselves to discharge the duties which devolve on them in their respective offices. The offices of Secretary and Treasurer, are by some considered the most important in the Lodge, particularly where there is much business done.]

I will now introduce the reader to the second degree of Masonry. It is generally called passing, as will be seen in the lecture. I shall omit the ceremonies of opening and closing, as they are precisely the same as in the first degree, except two knocks are used in this degree, and the door is entered by the benefit of a pass-word; it is *Shibboleth*. It will be explained in the lecture.

The Candidate, as before, is taken into the preparation room and prepared in the manner following; all his clothing taken off except his shirt; furnished with a pair of drawers; his right breast bare; his left foot in a slipper, the right bare; a Cable-Tow twice round his neck; semi-hoodwinked; in which situation he is conducted to the door of the Lodge, where he gives two knocks, when the Senior Warden rises and says, 'Worshipful, while we are peaceably at work on the second degree of Masonry, under the influence of faith, hope, and charity, the door of our Lodge is alarmed.' Master to Junior Deacon, 'Brother Junior, inquire the cause of that alarm.' [In many Lodges they come to the door, knock, are answered by the Junior Deacon, and come in without their being noticed by the Senior Warden or Master.] The Junior Deacon gives two raps on the inside of the door. The Candidate gives one without; it is answered by the Junior Deacon with one, when the door is partly opened by the Junior Deacon, who inquires, 'Who comes here? who comes here?' The Senior Deacon, who is or ought to be, the conductor, answers, 'A worthy Brother who has been regularly initiated as an Entered Apprentice Mason, served a proper time as such, and now wishes for further light in Masonry by being passed to the degree of Fellow-Craft.' Junior Deacon to Senior Deacon, 'Is it of his own free will and accord he makes this request?' *Ans.* 'It is.' Junior Deacon to Senior Deacon, 'Is he duly and truly prepared?' *Ans.* 'He is.' Junior Deacon to Senior Deacon, 'Is he worthy and well qualified?' *Ans.* 'He is.' Junior Deacon to Senior Deacon, 'Has he made suitable proficiency in the preceding degree?' *Ans.* 'He has.' [Very few know any more than they did the night they were initiated; have not heard their obligation repeated, nor one section of the Lecture, and in fact a very small proportion of Masons ever learn either.] Junior Deacon to Senior Deacon, 'By what further rights does he expect to obtain this benefit? *Ans.* 'By the benefit of a pass-word.' Junior Deacon to Senior Deacon, *'Has he a pass-word?'* *Ans.* 'He has not, but I have it for him.' Junior Deacon to Senior Deacon, 'Give it to me.' The Senior Deacon whispers in the Junior Deacon's ear, *Shibboleth*. The Junior Deacon says, 'The pass is right; since this is the case, you will wait until the Worshipful Master in the East is made acquainted with his request, and his answer returned.' The Junior Deacon then repairs to the Master and gives two knocks, as at the door, which are answered by two, by the Master when the same questions are asked and answers returned as at the door after which the Master says, 'Since he comes indued with all these necessary qualifications, let him enter this Worshipful Lodge in the name of the Lord, and take heed on what he enters.' As he enters, the angle of the square is pressed hard against his naked right breast, at which time the Junior Deacon says, 'Brother, when you entered this Lodge the first time, you entered on the point of the compass pressing your naked left breast, which was then explained to you. You now enter it on the angle of the square, pressing your naked right breast, which is to teach you to act upon the square with all mankind, but more especially with the Brethren.' The Candidate is then conducted twice regularly round the Lodge, and halted at the Junior Warden in the South, where he gives two raps, and is answered by two, when the same questions are asked and answers returned as at the door; from thence he is conducted to the Senior Warden, where the same questions are asked and answers returned as before; he is then conducted to the Master in the East, where the same questions are asked and answers returned as before; the Master likewise demands of him, from whence he came, and whither he was traveling; he answers, 'From the West and traveling to the East.' The Master asks, 'Why do you leave the West and travel to the East?' *Ans.* 'In search of more light.' The Master then says to the Candidate, 'Since this is the case, you will please conduct the Candidate back to the West, from whence he came, and put him in care of the Senior Warden, who will teach him how to approach the East, ' The place of light,' by advancing upon two upright regular steps to the second step [his heel is in the hollow of the right foot on this degree], his feet forming the right angle of an oblong square, and his body erect at the altar before the Worshipful Master, and place him in a proper position to take the solemn oath, or obligation of a Fellow-Craft Mason. The Master then leaves his seat and approaches the kneeling Candidate [the Candidate kneels on the right knee, the left forming a square, his left arm as far as the elbow in a horizontal position, and the rest of the arm in a vertical position, so as to form a square, his arm supported by the square held under his elbow], and says, 'Brother, you are now placed in a proper position to take on you the solemn oath, or obligation of Fellow-Craft Mason, which, I assure you, as before, is neither to affect your religion nor politics: if you are willing to take it, repeat your name and say after me,—

'I, A. B., of my own free will and accord, in the presence of Almighty God, and this Worshipful Lodge of Fellow-Craft Masons, dedicated to God, and held forth to the holy order of St. John, do hereby and hereon most solemnly and sincerely promise, and swear, in addition to my former obligation, that I will not give the degree of a Fellow-Craft Mason to any one of an inferior degree, nor to any other being in the known world, except it be to a true and lawful Brother, or Brethren Fellow-Craft Masons, or within the body of a just and lawfully constituted Lodge of such; and not unto him nor unto them whom I shall hear so to be, but unto him and them only whom I shall find so to be, after strict trial and due examination, or lawful information. Furthermore do I promise and swear, that I will not wrong this Lodge, nor a Brother of this degree, to the value of two cents knowingly, myself, nor suffer it to be done by others if in my power to prevent it. Furthermore do I promise and swear, that I will support the Constitution of the Grand Lodge of the United States, and of the Grand Lodge of this State, under which this Lodge is held, and conform to all the by-laws, rules, and regulations of this or any other Lodge, of which I may at any time hereafter become a member, as far as in my power. Furthermore do I promise, and swear, that I will obey all regular signs and summons' given, handed, sent, or thrown to me by the hand of a Brother Fellow-Craft Mason, or from the body of a just and lawfully constituted Lodge, of such, provided that it be within the length of my Cable-Tow, or square and angle of my work. Furthermore do I promise, and swear, that I will be aiding and assisting all poor and penniless Brethren Fellow-Crafts, their widows and orphans wheresoever disposed round the globe, they applying to me as such, as far as in my power without injuring myself or family. To all which I do most solemnly and sincerely promise, and swear, without the least hesitation, mental reservation, or self-evasion of mind in me whatever, binding myself under no less penalty than to have my left breast torn open, and my heart and vitals taken from thence and thrown over my left shoulder and carried into the valley of Jehosaphat, there to become a prey to the wild beasts of the field and vultures of the air, if ever I should prove willfully guilty of violating any part of this my solemn oath, or obligation of a Fellow-Craft Mason; so keep me God, and keep me steadfast in the due performance of the same.' 'Detach your hands and kiss the book, which is the Holy Bible, twice.' The bandage is now (by one of the Brethren) dropped over the other eye, and the Master says, 'Brother [at the same time laying his hand on the top of the Candidate's head], what do you most desire?' the Candidate answers after his prompter, 'More light.' The Master says, 'Brethren, form on the square and assist in bringing our new made Brother from darkness to light: 'And God said, let there be light, and there was light.' At this instant all the Brethren clap their hands and stamp on the floor as in the preceding degree. The Master says to the Candidate, 'Brother, what do you discover different from before?' The Master says, after a short pause, 'You now discover one point of the compass elevated above the square, which denotes light in this degree; but as one is yet in obscurity, it is to remind you that you are yet one material point in the dark, respecting Masonry.' The Master steps off from the Candidate three or four steps, and says, 'Brother, you now discover me as Master of the Lodge, approaching you from the East, under the sign and due-guard of a Fellow-Craft Mason, do as I do, as near as you can, and keep your position.' The sign is given by drawing your right-hand flat, with the palm of it next to your breast, across your breast from the left to the right side with some quickness, and dropping it down by your side; the due-guard is given by raising the left arm until that part of it between the elbow and shoulder is perfectly horizontal, and raising the rest of the arm in a vertical position, so that that part of the arm below the elbow, and that part above it, form a square. This is called the due-guard of a Fellow-Craft Mason. The two given together, are called the sign and due-guard of a Fellow-Craft Mason, and they are never given separately; they would not be recognized by a Mason if given separately. The Master, by the time he gives his steps, sign, and due-guard, arrives at the Candidate, and says,

'Brother, I now present you with my right-hand in token of Brotherly love and confidence, and with it the pass-grip and word of a Fellow-Craft Mason.' The pass, or more properly the pass-grip, is given by taking each other by the right-hand as though going to shake hands, and each putting his thumb between the fore and second fingers where they join the hand, and pressing the thumb between the joints. This is the pass-grip of a Fellow-Craft Mason, the name of it is *Shibboleth*. Its origin will be explained in the lecture—the pass-grip some give without lettering or syllabling, and others give it in the same way they do the real grip; the real grip of a Fellow-Craft Mason is given by putting the thumb on the joint of the second finger where it joins the hand, and crooking your thumb so that each can stick the nail of his thumb into the joint of the other; this is the real grip of a Fellow-Craft Mason; the name of it is *Jachin;* it is given in the following manner: If you wish to examine a person, after having taken each other by the grip, ask him, 'What is this?' *Ans.* 'A grip,' *Q.* 'A grip of what? *Ans.* 'The grip of a Fellow-Craft Mason.' *Q.* 'Has it a name?' *Ans.* 'It has.' *Q.* 'Will you give it to me? *Ans.* 'I did not so receive it, neither can I so impart it.' *Q.* 'What will you do with it?' *Ans.* 'I'll letter it or halve it.' *Q.* 'Halve it and you begin?' *Ans.* 'No, begin you.' *Q.* 'You begin?' *Ans.* 'J-A.' *Q.* 'C-H-I-N.' *Ans.* 'JACHIN.' *Q.* 'Right, Brother *Jachin*, I greet you.'

As the signs, due-guards, grips, pass-grips, words, pass-words, and their several names comprise pretty much all the secrets of Masonry, and *all* the information necessary to pass us as Masons, I intend to appropriate a few passages in the latter part of this work, to the exclusive purpose of explaining them; I shall not, therefore, spend much time in examining them as I progress.—After the Master gives the Candidate the pass-grip and grip, and their names, he says, 'Brother, you will rise and salute the Junior and Senior Wardens as such, and convince them that you have been regularly passed to the degree of a Fellow-Craft Mason, and have got the sign and pass-grip, real grip, and their names.' [I do not here express it as expressed in Lodges generally: the Master generally says, 'You will arise and salute the Wardens, &c. and convince them, &c. that you have got the sign, pass-grip and word.' It is obviously wrong, because the first thing he gives is the sign, then due-guard, then the pass-grip, real grip, and their names] While the Wardens are examining the Candidate, the Master gets an apron and returns to the Candidate and says, 'Brother, I now have the honor of presenting you with a lamb-skin or white apron as before, which I hope you will continue to wear with honor to yourself and satisfaction to the Brethren; you will please carry it to the Senior Warden in the West, who will teach you how to wear it as a Fellow-Craft Mason.'—The Senior Warden ties on his apron and turns up one corner of the lower end of the apron and tucks it under the apron string. The Senior Deacon then conducts his pupil to the Master, who has by this time resumed his seat in the East, where he has, or ought to have, the floor carpeted to assist him in his explanations. Master to the Candidate, 'Brother, as you are dressed, it is necessary you should have tools to work with, I will therefore present you with the tools of a Fellow-Craft Mason. They are the plumb, square and level. The plumb is an instrument made use of by operative Masons to raise perpendiculars; the square to square their work; and the level to lay horizontals; but we, as Free and Accepted Masons, are taught to use them for more noble and glorious purposes; the plumb teaches us to walk uprightly in our several stations before God and man, squaring our actions by the square of virtue, and remembering that we are traveling on the level of time to that undiscovered country from whose bourn no traveler has returned. I further present you with these precious jewels; their names are Faith, Hope, and Charity; they teach us to have faith in God, hope in immortality, and charity to all mankind.' The Master to the Senior Deacon, 'You will now conduct the Candidate out of the Lodge, and invest him with what he has been divested.' After he is clothed, and the necessary arrangements made for his reception, such as placing the columns and floor-carpet, if they have any, the Candidate is re-conducted back to the Lodge; as he enters the door the Senior Deacon observes, 'We are now about to return to the middle chamber of King Solomon's Temple.' When within the door the Senior Deacon proceeds, 'Brother, we have worked in speculative and operative Masonry; they worked at the building of King Solomon's Temple, and many other Masonic edifices, they wrought six days, they did not work on the seventh, because in six days God created the heavens and earth and rested on the seventh day—the seventh therefore our ancient Brethren consecrated as a day of rest, thereby enjoying more frequent opportunities to contemplate the glorious works of creation, and to adore their great Creator.' Moving a step or two the Senior Deacon proceeds, 'Brother, the first thing that attracts our attention, are two large columns, or pillars, one on the left-hand and the other on the right; the name of the one on the left-hand is Boaz, and denotes strength, the name of the one on the right-hand is Jachin, and denotes establishment; they collectively allude to a passage in Scripture, wherein God hath declared in his word, 'In strength shall this House be established.' These columns are eighteen cubits high, twelve in circumference, and four in diameter; they are adorned with two large Chapiters, one on each, and these Chapiters, are ornamented with net-work, lily-work, and pomegranates; they denote unity, peace, and plenty. The net-work, from its connection, denotes union; the lily-work, from its whitness, purity and peace; and the pomegranate, from the exuberance of its seed, denotes plenty. They also have two large globes or balls, one on each; these globes or balls contain on their convex surfaces all the maps and charts of the celestial and terrestrial bodies; they are said to be thus extensive, to denote the universality of

Masonry, and that a Mason's charity ought to be equally extensive. Their composition is molten, or cast brass, they were cast on the banks of the river Jordan, in the clay-ground between Succoth, and Zaradatha, where King Solomon ordered these and all other holy vessels to be cast; they were cast hollow; and were four inches or a hand's breadth thick; they were cast hollow the better to withstand inundations and conflagrations—were the archives of Masonry; and contained the constitution, rolls, and records. The Senior Deacon having explained the columns, he passes between them, advancing a step or two, observing as he advances, 'Brother, we will pursue our travels; the next thing that we come to, is a long winding staircase, with three, five, seven steps or more. The three first allude to the three principal supports in Masonry, viz: wisdom, strength, and beauty; the five steps allude to the five orders in architecture, and the five human senses; the five orders in architecture, are, the Tuscan, Doric, Ionic, Corinthian, and Composite; the five human senses, are, hearing, seeing, feeling, smelling and tasting; the three first of which, have ever been highly essential among Masons; hearing, to hear the word, seeing to see the sign, and feeling to feel the grip, whereby one Mason may know another in the dark as well as in the light. The seven steps allude to the seven sabbatical years, seven years of famine, seven years in building the Temple, seven golden candlesticks, seven wonders of the world; seven planets, but more especially the several liberal arts and sciences, which are grammar, rhetoric, logic, arithmetic, geometry, music, and astronomy: for this and many other reasons, the number seven has ever been held in high estimation among Masons.' Advancing a few steps, the Senior Deacon proceeds; 'Brother, the next thing we come to is the outer door of the middle chamber of King Solomon's Temple, which is partly open, but closely Tyled by the Junior Warden.' [It is the Junior Warden in the South who represents the Tyler at the outer door of the middle chamber of King Solomon's Temple], who, on the approach of the Senior Deacon and candidate, inquires, 'Who comes here, who comes here?' The Senior Deacon answers, 'A Fellow-Craft Mason.' Junior Warden to Senior Deacon, 'How do you expect to gain admission?' *A.* 'By a pass and token of a pass.' Junior Warden to Senior Deacon, 'Will you give them to me?' The Senior Deacon (or the Candidate, prompted by him) gives them; this and many other tokens or grips, are frequently given by strangers, when first introduced to each other; if given to a Mason he will immediately return it; they can be given in any company unobserved, even by Masons, when shaking hands. *A pass and token of a pass:* the pass is the word *Shibboleth;* the token, alias the pass-grip, is given as before described, by taking each other by the right-hand as if in shaking hands, and placing the thumb between the fore finger and second finger at the third joint, or where they join the hand, and pressing it hard enough to attract attention. In the lecture it is called a token, but generally called the pass-grip; it is an undeniable fact that Masons express themselves so differently, when they mean the same thing, that they frequently wholly misunderstand each other.]

After the Junior Warden has received the pass *Shibboleth*, he inquires, 'What does it denote?' Ans. 'Plenty.'—Junior Warden to Senior Deacon, 'Why so?' Ans. 'From an ear of corn being placed at the water-ford.' Junior Warden to Senior Deacon, 'Why was this pass instituted?' Ans. 'In consequence of a quarrel which had long existed between Jeptha, judge of Israel, and the Ephraimites, the latter of whom had long been a stubborn, rebellious people, whom Jeptha had endeavored to subdue by lenient measures, but to no effect. The Ephraimites being highly incensed against Jeptha for not being called to fight, and share in the rich spoils of the Ammonitish war, assembled a mighty army, and passed over the river Jordan to give Jeptha battle; but he being apprised of their approach, called together the men of Israel, and gave them battle, and put them to flight; and, to make his victory more complete, he ordered guards to be placed at the different passes on the banks of the river Jordan, and commanded, if the Ephraimites passed that way, that they should pronounce the word *Shibboleth;* but they, being of a different tribe, pronounced it Seboleth, which trifling defect proved them spies, and cost them their lives: and there fell that day, at the different passes on the banks of the river Jordan, forty and two thousand. This word was also used by our ancient brethren to distinguish a friend from a foe, and has since been adopted as a proper pass-word, to be given before entering any well-regulated and governed Lodge of Fellow-Craft Masons.' 'Since this is the case, you will pass on to the Senior Warden in the West, for further examination.' As they approach the Senior Warden in the West, the Senior Deacon says to the Candidate, 'Brother, the next thing we come to is the inner door of the middle chamber of King Solomon's Temple, which we find partly open, but more closely tyled by the Senior Warden, when the Senior Warden inquires, 'Who comes here? who comes here?' The Senior Deacon answers, 'A Fellow-Craft Mason.' Senior Warden to Senior Deacon, 'How do you expect to gain admission?' Ans. 'By the grip and word.' The Senior Warden to the Junior Deacon, 'Will you give them to me?' They are then given as hereinbefore described. The word is *Jachin*. After they are given, the Senior Warden says, 'They are right; you can pass on to the Worshipful Master in the East. As they approach the Worshipful Master, he inquires, 'Who comes here? who comes here?' Junior Deacon answers, 'A Fellow-Craft Mason.' The Master then says to the Candidate, 'Brother, you have been admitted into the middle chamber of King Solomon's Temple, for the sake of the letter G. It denotes Deity, before whom we all ought to bow with reverence, worship and adore. It also denotes Geometry, the fifth science, it being that on which this degree was principally founded. By Geometry we may curiously trace nature through her various windings to her most concealed recesses: by it, we may discover the power, the wisdom, and the goodness of the grand Artificer of the Universe, and view with delight the proportions which connect this vast Machine: by it, we may discover how the planets move in their different orbits, and demonstrate their various revolutions: by it, we account for the return of seasons, and the variety of scenes which each season displays to the discerning eye. Numberless worlds surround us, all formed by the same divine Architect, which roll through this vast expanse, and all conducted by the same unerring law of nature. A survey of nature, and the observations of her beautiful proportions, first determined man to imitate the divine plan, and study symmetry and order The Architect began to design; and the plans which he laid down, being improved by experience and time, have produced works which are the admiration of every age. The lapse of time, the ruthless hand of ignorance, and the devastations of war have laid waste and destroyed many valuable monuments of antiquity, on which the utmost exertion of human genius has been employed. Even the Temple of Solomon, so spacious and magnificent, and constructed by so many celebrated artists, escaped not the unsparing ravages of barbarous force. The *attentive ear* receives the sound from the *instructive tongue*, and the mysteries of Free Masonry are safely lodged in the repository of *faithful breasts*. Tools and implements of architecture, and symbolic emblems, most expressive, are selected by the fraternity, to imprint on the mind wise and serious truths; and thus, through a succession of ages, are transmitted, unimpaired, the most excellent tenets of our institution.' Here ends the work part of the Fellow-Craft's degree. It will be observed that the Candidate has received, in this place, the second section of the lecture on this degree. This course is not generally pursued, but it is much the most instructive method, and when it is omitted, I generally conclude that it is for want of a knowledge of the lecture. Monitorial writers (who are by no means coeval with Masonry), all write or copy very much after each other, and they have all inserted in their books all those clauses of the several lectures which are not considered by the wise ones as tending to develop the secrets of Masonry. In some instances, they change the phraseology a little; in others, they are literal extracts from the lectures. This, it is said, is done to facilitate the progress of learners, or young Masons, when in fact, it has the contrary effect. All lecture teachers (and there are many traveling about the country, with recommendations from some of their distinguished brethren), when they come to any of those clauses, will say to their pupils, 'I have not committed that, it is in the Monitor, you can learn it at your leisure.' This course of procedure subjects the learner to the necessity of making his own questions, and, of course, answering monitorially, whether the extracts from the lectures are literal or not. Again, there is not a *perfect* sameness in all the Monitors, or they could not all get copyrights; hence the great diversity in the lectures as well as the work. The following charge is, or ought to be, delivered to the Candidate after he has got through the ceremonies; but he is generally told, 'It is in the Monitor, and you can read it at your leisure:'

'Brother, being advanced to the second degree of Masonry, we congratulate you on your preferment. The internal, and not the external, qualifications of a man, are what Masonry regards. As you increase in knowledge, you will improve in social intercourse.

'It is unnecessary to recapitulate the duties which, as a Mason, you are bound to discharge; or enlarge on the necessity of a strict adherence to them, as your own experience must have established their value.

'Our laws and regulations you are strenuously to support; and be always ready to assist in seeing them duly executed. You are not to palliate or aggravate the offenses of your brethren; but in the decision of every trespass against our rules, you are to judge with candor, admonish with friendship, and reprehend with justice.

'The study of the liberal arts, that valuable branch of education, which tends so effectually to polish and adorn the mind, is earnestly recommended to your consideration; especially the science of Geometry, which is established as the basis of our art. Geometry, or Masonry, originally synonymous terms, being of a divine moral nature, is enriched with the most useful knowledge; while it proves the wonderful properties of nature, it demonstrates the more important truths of morality.

'Your past behavior and regular deportment have merited the honor which we have now conferred; and in your new character it is expected that you will conform to the principles of the Order, by steadily persevering in the practice of every commendable virtue.

'Such is the nature of your engagements as a Fellow-Craft, and to these duties you are bound by the most sacred ties.'

I will now proceed with the Lectures on this degree. It is divided into two sections.

SECTION FIRST.

Q. Are you a Fellow-Craft Mason?
A. I am—try me.
Q. By what will you be tried?
A. By the square.
Q. Why by the square?
A. Because it is an emblem of virtue.
Q. What is a square?
A. An angle extending to ninety degrees, or the fourth part of a circle.

Q. Where was you prepared to be made a Fellow-Craft Mason?

A. In a room adjacent to the body of a just and lawfully constituted Lodge of such, duly assembled in a room or place, representing the middle chamber of king Solomon's Temple.

Q. How was you prepared?

A. By being divested of all metals; neither naked nor clothed; barefoot nor shod; hoodwinked; with a cable-tow twice round my neck; in which situation I was conducted to the door of the Lodge, where I gave two distinct knocks.

Q. What did those two distinct knocks allude to?

A. The second degree in Masonry, it being that on which I was about to enter.

Q. What was said to you from within?

A. Who comes here? who comes here?

Q. Your answer?

A. A worthy Brother who has been regularly initiated as an Entered Apprentice Mason; served a proper time as such, and now wishes for further light in Masonry by being passed to the degree of a Fellow-Craft.

Q. What was then said to you from within?

A. I was asked if it was of my own free will and accord I made this request; if I was duly and truly prepared; worthy and well qualified, and had made suitable proficiency in the preceding degree; all of which being answered in the affirmative, I was asked, by what further rights I expected to obtain so great a benefit.

Q. Your answer?

A. By the benefit of a pass-word.

Q. What is that pass-word? *A. Shibboleth.*

Q. What further was said to you from within?

A. I was bid to wait until the Worshipful Master in the East was made acquainted with my request, and his answer returned.

Q. After his answer was returned, what followed?

A. I was caused to enter the Lodge.

Q. How did you enter?

A. On the angle of the square presented to my naked right breast in the name of the Lord.

Q. How was you then disposed of?

A. I was conducted twice regularly round the Lodge, and halted at the Junior Warden in the South, where the same questions were asked and answers returned as at the door.

Q. How did the Junior Warden dispose of you?

A. He ordered me to be conducted to the Senior Warden in the West, where the same questions were asked, and answers returned as before.

Q. How did the Senior Warden dispose of you?

A. He ordered me to be conducted to the Worshipful Master in the East, where the same questions were asked, and answers returned as before, who likewise demanded of me from whence I came, and whither I was traveling.

Q. Your answer?

A. From the West, and traveling to the East.

Q. Why do you leave the West and travel to the East?

A. In search of more light.

Q. How did the Worshipful Master then dispose of you?

A. He ordered me to be conducted back to the West, from whence I came, and put in care of the Senior Warden, who taught me how to approach the East, by advancing upon two upright, regular steps to the second step, my feet forming the right angle of an oblong square, and my body erect at the altar before the Worshipful Master.

Q. What did the Worshipful Master do with you?

A. He made a Fellow-Craft Mason of me.

Q. How? A. In due form.

Q. What was that due form?

A. My right knee bare. bent, my left knee forming a square, my right hand on the Holy Bible, square and compass, my left arm forming an angle supported by the square, and my hand in a vertical position, in which posture I took upon me the solemn oath or obligation of a Fellow-Craft Mason. [See page 33 for obligation.]

Q. After your oath or obligation, what was said to you?

A. I was asked what I most desired.

Q. Your answer? A. More light.

Q. On being brought to light, what did you discover different from before?

A. One point of the compass elevated above the square, which denoted light in this degree, but as one point was yet in obscurity, it was to remind me that I was yet one material point in the dark respecting Masonry.

Q. What did you next discover?

A. The Worshipful Master approaching me from the East, under the sign and due-guard of a Fellow-Craft Mason, who presented me with his right-hand in token of brotherly love and confidence, and proceeded to give me the pass-grip and word of a Fellow-Craft Mason, and bid me rise and salute the Junior and Senior Wardens, and convince them that I had been regularly passed to the degree of a Fellow-Craft, and had the sign, grip, and word of a Fellow-Craft Mason.

Q. What did you next discover?

A. The Worshipful Master approaching me a second time from the East, who presented me with a lamb-skin, or white apron, which he said he hoped I would continue to wear with honor to myself, and satisfaction and advantage to the brethren.

Q. What was you next presented with?

A. The working-tools of a Fellow-Craft Mason.

Q. What are they?

A. The Plumb, Square, and Level.

Q. What do they teach? (I think this question ought to be, 'How explained?')

A. The Plumb is an instrument made use of by operative Masons to raise perpendiculars; the Square, to square their work; and the Level to lay horizontals; but we, as Free and Accepted Masons, are taught to make use of them for more noble and glorious purposes: the Plumb admonishes us to walk uprightly in our several stations before God and man, squaring our actions by the square of virtue, and remembering that we are all traveling upon the level of time to that undiscovered country from whose bourn no traveler returns.

Q. What was you next presented with?

A. Three precious jewels.

Q. What were they? A. Faith, Hope, and Charity.

Q. What do they teach?

A. Faith in God, hope in immortality, and charity to all mankind.

Q. How was you then disposed of?

A. I was conducted out of the Lodge, and invested of what I had been divested.

SECOND SECTION.

Q. Have you ever worked as a Fellow-Craft Mason?

A. I have, in speculative; but our forefathers wrought both in speculative and operative Masonry.

Q. Where did they work?

A. At the building of King Solomon's Temple, and many other Masonic edifices.

Q. How long did they work? A. Six days.

Q. Did they not work on the seventh?

A. They did not.

Q. Why so?

A. Because in six days God created the Heavens and the Earth, and rested on the seventh day; the seventh day, therefore, our ancient brethren consecrated as a day of rest from their labors; thereby enjoying more frequent opportunities to contemplate the glorious works of creation, and adore their great Creator!

Q. Did you ever return to the sanctum sanctorum, or holy of holies of King Solomon's Temple?

A. I did. Q. By what way?

A. Through a long porch or alley.

Q. Did anything particular strike your attention on your return?

A. There did, viz: two large columns, or pillars, one on the left-hand and the other on the right.

Q. What was the name of the one on your left-hand?

A. *Boaz*, to denote strength.

Q. What was the name of the one on your right-hand?

A. *Jachin*, denoting establishment.

Q. What do they collectively allude to?

A. A passage in Scripture wherein God has declared in his word, 'In strength shall this House be established.'

Q. What were their dimensions?

A. Eighteen cubits in hight, twelve in circumference, and four in diameter

Q. Were they adorned with anything?

A. They were, with two large Chapiters, one on each.

Q. Were they ornamented with anything?

A. They were with wreaths of net-work, lily-work and pomegranates.

Q. What do they denote?

A. Unity, peace and plenty.   Q. Why so?

A. Net-work, from its connection, denotes union; lily-work, from its whiteness and purity, denotes peace; and the pomegranate, from the exuberance of its seed, denotes plenty.

Q. Were those columns adorned with anything further?

A. They were, viz: two large globes or balls, one on each.

Q. Did they contain any thing?

A. They did, viz: All the maps and charts of the celestial and terrestrial bodies.

Q. Why are they said to be so extensive?

A. To denote the universality of Masonry, and that a Mason's charity ought to be equally extensive.

Q. What was their composition?

A. Molten, or cast brass.   Q. Who cast them?

A. Our Grand Master, Hiram Abiff.

Q. Where were they cast?

A. On the banks of the river Jordan, in the clay-ground between Succoth and Zaradatha, where King Solomon ordered these and all other Holy vessels to be cast.

Q. Were they cast sound, or hollow?   *A.* Hollow.

Q. What was their thickness?

A. Four inches, or a hand's-breadth.

Q. Why were they cast hollow?

A. The better to withstand inundations and conflagrations; were the archives of Masonry, and contained the constitution, rolls and records.

Q. What did you next come to?

A. A long winding staircase, with three, five, seven steps or more.

Q. What do the three steps allude to?

A. The three principal supports in Masonry, viz: wisdom, strength, and beauty.

Q. What do the five steps allude to?

A. The five orders in architecture, and the five human senses.

Q. What are the five orders in architecture?

A. The Tuscan, Doric, Ionic, Corinthian, and Composite.

Q. What are the five human senses?

A. Hearing, seeing, feeling, smelling, and tasting; the first three of which nave ever been deemed highly essential among Masons; hearing, to hear the word; seeing, to see the sign; and feeling, to feel the grip, whereby one Mason may know another in the dark, as well as in the light.

Q. What do the seven steps allude to?

A. The seven sabbatical years, seven years of famine, seven years in building the Temple, seven golden candlesticks, seven wonders of the world, seven planets; but more especially the seven liberal arts and sciences, which are grammar, rhetoric, logic, arithmetic, geometry, music, and astronomy. For these, and many other reasons, the number seven has ever been held in high estimation among Masons.

Q. What did you next come to?

A. The outer door of the middle chamber of King Solomon's Temple, which I found partly open, but closely tyled by the Junior Warden.

Q. How did you gain admission?

A. By a pass, and token of a pass.

Q. What was the name of the pass? A. *Shibboleth*.

Q. What does it denote? A. Plenty. Q. Why so?

A. From an ear of corn being placed at the water-ford.

Q. Why was this pass instituted?

A. In consequence of a quarrel which had long existed between Jeptha, judge of Israel, and the Ephraimites; the latter of whom had long been a stubborn, rebellious people, whom Jeptha had endeavored to subdue by lenient measures; but to no effect. The Ephraimites being highly incensed against Jeptha, for not being called to fight and share in the rich spoils of the Ammonitish war, assembled a mighty army, and passed over the river Jordan to give Jeptha battle; but he, being apprised of their approach, called together the men of Israel, and gave them battle, and put them to flight; and to make his victory more complete, he ordered guards to be placed at the different passes on the banks of the river Jordan, and commanded, if the Ephraimites passed that way, that they should pronounce the word *Shibboleth;* but they, being of a different tribe, pronounced it *Seboleth;* which trifling defect proved them spies, and cost them their lives; and there fell that day at the different passes on the banks of the river Jordan, forty and two thousand. This word was also used by our ancient brethren to distinguish a friend from a foe, and has since been

D

adopted as a proper pass-word to be given before entering any well-regulated and governed Lodge of Fellow-Craft Masons.

Q. What did you next come to?

A. The inner door of the middle chamber of King Solomon's Temple, which I found partly open, but closely tyled by the Senior Warden.

Q. How did you gain admittance?

A. By the grip and word.

Q. How did the Senior Warden dispose of you?

A. He ordered me to be conducted to the Worshipful Master in the East, who informed me that I had been admitted into the middle chamber of King Solomon's Temple for the sake of the letter G.

Q. Does it denote anything?

A. It does: DEITY, before whom we should all bow with reverence, worship and adore. It also denotes Geometry, the fifth science; it being that on which this degree was principally founded.

Thus ends the second degree of Masonry.

THE THIRD, OR MASTER-MASON'S DEGREE.

THE traditional account of the death, several burials, and resurrection of Hiram Abiff, the widow's son [as hereafter narrated], admitted as facts, this degree is certainly very interesting. The Bible informs us, that there was a person of that name employed at the building of King Solomon's Temple; but neither the Bible, the writings of Josephus, nor any other writings, however ancient, of which I have any knowledge, furnish any information respecting his death. It certainly is very singular, that a man so celebrated as Hiram Abiff, who was an arbiter between Solomon, king of Israel, and Hiram, king of Tyre, universally acknowledged as the third most distinguished man then living, and in many respects the greatest man in the world, should pass off the stage of action in the presence of king Solomon, three thousand three hundred grand overseers, and one hundred and fifty thousand workmen, with whom he had spent a number of years, and neither king Solomon, his bosom friend, nor any other among his numerous friends ever recorded his death or anything about him. I make these remarks now, hoping that they may induce some person who has time and capacity to investigate the subject, and promulgate the result of their investigations. I shall let the subject rest where it is at present; it is not intended that it should form any part of this little volume. The principal object of this work is to lay before the world a true history of Free Masonry, without saying anything for or against it.

A person who has received the two preceding degrees, and wishes to be raised to the sublime degree of a Master-Mason, is then [the Lodge being opened as in the preceding degrees] conducted from the preparation room to the door [the manner of preparing him is particularly explained in the lecture], where he gives three distinct knocks, when the Senior Warden rises and says, 'Worshipful, while we are peaceably at work on the third degree of Masonry, under the influence of humanity, Brotherly love, and affection, the door of our Lodge appears to be alarmed.' The Master to the Junior Deacon, 'Brother Junior, inquire the cause of that alarm. The Senior Deacon then steps to the door, and answers the three knocks that had been given, by three more [these knocks are much louder than those given on any occasion, other than that of the admission of Candidates in the several degrees]; one knock is then given without, and answered by one from within, when the door is partly opened, and the Junior asks, 'Who comes there? who comes there? who comes there?' The Senior Deacon answers, 'A worthy Bro ther, who has been regularly initiated as an Entered Apprentice Mason, passed to the degree of a Fellow-Craft, and now wishes for further light in Masonry, by being raised to the sublime degree of a Master-Mason.' Junior Deacon to Senior Deacon, 'Is it of his own free will and accord, he makes this request? *Ans.* 'It is.' Junior Deacon to Senior Deacon, 'Is he duly and truly prepared?' *Ans.* 'He is.' Junior Deacon to Senior Deacon, 'Is he worthy and well qualified?' *Ans.* 'He is.' Junior Deacon to Senior Deacon, 'Has he made suitable proficiency in the preceding degrees?' *Ans.* 'He has.' Junior Deacon to Senior Deacon, 'By what further rights does he expect to obtain this benefit?' *Ans.* 'By the benefit of a pass-word.' Junior Deacon to Senior Deacon, '*Has he a pass-word?*' *Ans.* 'He has not, but I have got it for him.' The Junior Deacon to Senior Deacon, 'Will you give it to me?' The Senior Deacon then whispers in the ear of the Junior Deacon, '*Tubal Cain.*' Junior Deacon says, 'The pass is right. Since this is the case you will wait until the Worshipful Master be made acquainted with his request and his answer returned.' The Junior Deacon then repairs to the Master and gives three knocks at the door; after answering which, the same questions are asked and answers returned, as at the door, when the Master says, 'Since he comes indued with all these necessary qualifications, let him enter this Worshipful Lodge in the name of the Lord, and take heed on what he enters.' The Junior Deacon returns to the door and says, 'Let him enter this Worshipful Lodge, in the name of the Lord, and take heed on what he enters.' In entering, both points of the compass are pressed against his naked right and left breasts, when the Junior Deacon stops the Candidate and says, 'Brother, when you first entered this Lodge, you was received on the point of the compass pressing your naked left breast, which was then explained to you; when you entered it the second time you was received on the angle of the square, which was also explained to you; on entering it now you are received on the two extreme points of the compass pressing your naked right and left breasts, which are thus explained: As the most vital parts of man are contained between the two breasts, so are the most valuable tenets of Masonry contained between the two extreme points of the compass, which are Virtue, Morality, and Brotherly love.' The Senior Deacon then conducts the Candidate three times regularly round the Lodge. [I wish the reader to observe, that on this, as well as every other degree, that the Junior Warden is the first of the three principal officers that the Candidate passes, traveling with the sun when he starts round the Lodge, and that as he passes the Junior Warden, Senior Warden, and Master, the first time going round, they each give one rap; the second time, two raps; and the third time, three raps each. The number of raps given on these occasions are the same as the number of the degree, except the first degree, on which three are given, I always thought improperly.] During the time the Candidate is traveling round the room, the Master reads the following passage of Scripture, the conductor and Candidate traveling, and the Master reading, so that the traveling and reading terminates at the same time: 'Remember now thy Creator in the days of thy youth, while the evil days come not, nor the years draw nigh, when thou shalt say, I have no pleasure in them; while the sun, or the light, or the moon, or the stars, be not darkened, nor the clouds return after the rain: in the day when the keepers of the house shall tremble, and the strong men shall bow themselves, and the grinders cease because they are few, and those that look out of the windows be darkened, and the doors shall be shut in the streets, when the sound of the grinding is low, and he shall rise up at the voice of the bird, and all the daughters of music shall be brought low. Also, when they shall be afraid of that which is high, and fears shall be in the way, and the almond tree shall flourish, and the grasshopper shall be a burden, and desire shall fail: because man goeth to his long home, and the mourners go about the streets; or even the silver cord be loosed, or the golden bowl be broken, or the pitcher be broken at the fountain, or the wheel at the cistern. Then shall the dust return to the earth as it was; and the spirit return unto God who gave it.' The conductor and Candidate halt at the Junior Warden in the South, where the same questions are asked and answers returned as at the door; he is then conducted to the Senior Warden in the West, where the same questions are asked and answers returned as before; from thence he is conducted to the W. Master in the East, who asks the same questions and receives the same answers as before, and who likewise asks the Candidate, from whence he came, and whither he is traveling. *Ans.* 'From the West, and traveling to the East.' *Q.* 'Why do you leave the West, and travel to the East?' *Ans.* 'In search of more light.' The Master then says to the Senior Deacon, 'You will please conduct the Candidate back to the West, from whence he came, and put him in care of the Senior Warden, and request him to teach the Candidate how to approach the East by advancing upon three upright regular steps to the third step, his feet forming a square, his body erect at the altar, before the Worshipful Master, and place him in a proper position to take upon him the solemn oath or obligation of a Master-Mason.' The Master then comes to the Candidate and says, 'Brother, you are now placed in a proper position [the lecture explains it] to take upon you the solemn oath or obligation of a Master-Mason, which, I assure you, as before, is neither to affect your religion nor politics. If you are willing to take it, repeat your name, and say after me :'

'I, A. B., of my own free will and accord, in presence of Almighty God, and this worshipful Lodge of Master-Masons, erected to God, and dedicated to the holy order of St. John, do hereby and hereon, most solemnly and sincerely promise and swear, in addition to my former obligations, that I will not give the degree of a Master-Mason, to any one of an inferior degree, nor to any other being in the known world, except it be to a true and lawful Brother or Brethren Master-Masons, or within the body of a just and lawfully constituted Lodge of such; and not unto him, nor unto them, whom I shall hear so to be, but unto him and them only whom I shall find so to be after strict trial and due examination, or lawful information received. Furthermore, do I promise and swear, that, I will not give the Master's word, which I shall hereafter receive, neither in the Lodge nor out of it; except it be on the five points of Fellowship and then not above my breath. Furthermore, do I promise and swear, that, I will not give the grand hailing sign of distress, except I am in real distress, or for the benefit of the Craft when at work; and should I ever see that sign given or the word accompanying it, and the person who gave it, appearing to be in distress, I will fly to his relief at the risk of my life, should there be a greater probability of saving his life, than losing my own. Furthermore, do I promise and swear, that, I will not wrong this Lodge, nor a Brother of this degree, to the value of one cent, knowingly, myself, nor suffer it to be done by others if in my power to prevent it. Furthermore, do I promise and swear, that, I will not be at the initiating, passing, and raising a Candidate at one communication, without a regular dispensation from the Grand Lodge for the same. Furthermore, do I promise and swear, that, I will not be at the initiating, passing, or raising a Candidate in a clandestine Lodge, I knowing it to be such. Furthermore, do I promise and swear, that, I will not be at the initiating of an old man in dotage, a young man in non-age, an Atheist, irreligious libertine, idiot, madman, hermaphrodite, nor woman. Furthermore, do I promise and swear, that, I will not speak evil of a Brother Master-Mason, neither behind his back nor before his face, but will apprize him of all approaching danger, if in my power. Furthermore, do I promise and swear, that, I will not violate the chastity of a Master-Mason's wife, mother, sister, or daughter, I knowing them to be such, nor suffer it to be done by others, if in my power to prevent it. Furthermore, do I promise and swear that, I will support the Constitution of the Grand Lodge of the state of ——— under which this Lodge is held, and conform to all the by-laws, rules and regulations of this, or any other Lodge of which I may at any time hereafter become a member. Furthermore, do I promise and swear, that, I will obey all regular signs, summons or tokens, given, handed, sent, or thrown to me from the hand of a Brother Master-Mason, or from the body of a just and lawfully constituted Lodge of such, provided it be within the length of my Cable-Tow. Furthermore, do I promise and swear, that, a Master-Mason's secrets, given to me in charge as such, and I knowing him to be such, shall remain as secure and inviolable in my breast, as in his own, when communicated to me, murder and treason excepted; and they left to my own election. Furthermore, do I promise and swear, that, I will go on a Master-Mason's errand whenever required, even should I have to go barefoot, and barehead, if within the length of my Cable-Tow. Furthermore, do I promise and swear, that, I will always remember a Brother Master-Mason, when on my knees offering up devotions to Almighty God. Furthermore, do I promise and swear, that, I will be aiding and assisting all poor, indigent Master-Masons, their wives and orphans, wheresoever disposed round the globe; as far as in my power, without injuring myself or family materially. Furthermore, do I promise and swear, that, if any part of this my solemn oath or obligation be omitted at this time, that I will hold myself amenable thereto whenever informed. To all which I do most solemnly and sincerely promise and swear, with a fixed and steady purpose of mind in me to keep, and perform the same, binding myself under no less penalty, than to have my body severed in two in the midst, and divided to the North and South, my bowels burnt to ashes in the center, and the ashes scattered before the four winds of heaven, that there might not the least tract or trace of remembrance remain among men or Masons of so vile and perjured a wretch as I should be, were I ever to prove willfully guilty of violating any part of this my solemn oath or obligation of a Master-Mason. So help me God, and keep me steadfast, in the due performance of the same.' The Master then asks the Candidate, 'What do you most desire?' The Candidate answers after his prompter, 'More Light.' The bandage, which was tied round his head in the preparation room, is, by one of the Brethren who stands behind him for that purpose, loosened and put over both eyes, and he is immediately brought to light in the same manner as in the preceding degree, except three stamps on the floor, and three claps of the hands are given in this degree. On being brought to light, the Master says to the Candidate, 'You first discover, as before, three great lights in Masonry by the assistance of three lesser, with this difference; both points of the compass, are elevated above the square, which denotes to you, that you are about to receive all the light that can be conferred on you in a Master's Lodge.' The Master steps back from the

Candidate and says, 'Brother, you now discover me, as Master of this Lodge, approaching you from the East, under the sign and due-guard of a Master-Mason.' The sign is given by raising both hands and arms to the elbows perpendicularly, one on either side of the head, the elbows forming a square. The words accompanying the sign in case of distress, are 'O Lord, my God, is there no help for the widow's son.' As the last words drop from your lips, you let your hands fall in that manner best calculated to indicate solemnity. King Solomon is said to have made this exclamation on the receipt of the information of the death of Hiram Abbiff. Masons are all charged never to give the *words*, except in the dark, when the sign cannot be seen. Here Masons differ very much; some contend that Solomon gave this sign, and made this exclamation when informed of Hiram's death, and work accordingly in their Lodges. Others say the sign was given and the exclamation made at the grave, when Solomon went there to raise Hiram, and of course they work accordingly; that is to say, the Master who governs a Lodge holding the latter opinion, gives the sign, &c. at the grave, when he goes to raise the body, and vice versa. The due-guard is given by putting the right-hand to the left side of the bowels, the hand open with the thumb next to the belly, and drawing it across the belly, and letting it fall; this is done tolerably quick. After the Master has given the sign and due-guard, 'which do not take more than a minute, he says, 'Brother, I now present you with my right-hand in token of Brotherly love and affection, and with it the pass-grip and word.' The pass-grip is given by pressing the thumb between the joints of the second and third fingers where they join the hand; the word or name is *Tubal Cain*. It is the pass-word to the Master's degree. The Master, after giving the Candidate the pass-grip and word, bids him rise and salute the Junior and Senior Wardens, and convince them that he is an obligated Master-Mason, and is in possession of the pass-grip and word. While the Wardens are examining the Candidate, the Master returns to the East and gets an apron, and as he returns to the Candidate, one of the Wardens, sometimes both, says to the Master, 'We are satisfied that Br. ———, is an obligated Master-Mason.' The Master then says to the Candidate, 'Brother, I now have the honor to present you with a lamb-skin or white apron, as before, which I hope you will continue to wear with credit to yourself, and satisfaction, and advantage to the Brethren; you will please carry it to the Senior Warden in the West, who will teach you how to wear it as a Master-Mason.

The Senior Warden ties on the apron, and lets the flap fall down before in its natural and common situation.

The Master returns to his seat and the Candidate is conducted to him. Master to Candidate, 'Brother, I perceive you are dressed, it is of course necessary you should have tools to work with. I will now present you with the working tools of a Master-Mason, and explain their uses to you. The trowel is an instrument made use of by operative masons to spread the cement which unites a building into one common mass; but we, as free and accepted Masons, are taught to make use of it for the more noble and glorious purpose of spreading the cement of *Brotherly love* and affection; that cement which unites us into one sacred band or society of friends and brothers among whom no contention should ever exist, but that noble contention or rather emulation of who can best work or best agree. I also present you with three precious jewels; their names are *humanity, friendship, and brotherly love.*

'Brother, you are not yet invested with all the secrets of this degree, nor do I know whether you ever will until I know how you withstand the amazing trials and dangers that await you.

'You are now about to travel to give us a specimen of your fortitude, perseverance, and fidelity in the preservation of what you have already received.—Fare you well, and may the Lord be with you, and support you through all your trials and difficulties.' [In some Lodges they make him pray before he starts.] The Candidate is then conducted out of the Lodge, clothed, and returns; as he enters the door, his conductor says to him, 'Brother, we are now in a place representing the *sanctum sanctorum, or holy of holies* of King Solomon's Temple. It was the custom of our Grand Master, Hiram Abbiff, every day at high twelve, when the Crafts were from labor to refreshment, to enter into the *sanctum sanctorum,* and offer up his devotions to the ever living God. Let us, in imitation of him, kneel and pray.' They then kneel, and the conductor says the following prayer: 'Thou, O God, knowest our downsitting and uprising, and understandest our thoughts afar off, shield and defend us, from the evil intentions of our enemies, and support us under the trials and afflictions we are destined to endure while traveling through this vale of tears. Man that is born of a woman, is of few days and full of trouble. He cometh forth as a flower, and is cut down; he fleeth also as a shadow, and continueth not. Seeing his days are determined, the number of his months are with thee, thou hast appointed his bounds, that he cannot pass; turn from him, that he may rest, until he shall accomplish his day. For there is hope of a tree, if it be cut down, that it will sprout again, and that the tender branch thereof will not cease. But man dieth and wasteth away; yea, man giveth up the ghost, and where is he? As the waters fail from the sea, and the flood decayeth and drieth up, so man lieth down, and riseth not up until the heavens shall be no more. Yet, O Lord! have compassion on the children of thy creation; administer unto them comfort in time of trouble, and save them with an everlasting salvation. Amen. So mote it be.' They then rise, and the conductor says to the Candidate, 'Brother, in further imitation of our Grand Master, Hiram Abbiff, let us retire at the South Gate.' They then advance to the Junior Warden [who represents *Jubela*, one of the ruffians] who exclaims, 'Who comes here?' [The room is dark or the Candidate hoodwinked], the conductor answers, 'Our Grand Master, Hiram Abbiff.' '*Our Grand Master, Hiram Abbiff!*' exclaims the ruffian, 'he is the very man I wanted to see.' Seizing the Candidate by the throat at the same time, and jerking him about with violence, 'Give me the Master-Mason's word, or I'll take your life.' The conductor replies, 'I cannot give it now, but if you will wait until the Grand Lodge assembles at Jerusalem, if you are found worthy, you shall then receive it, otherwise you cannot.' The ruffian then gives the Candidate a blow with the twenty-four inch gauge across the throat, on which he fled to the West gate; where he was accosted by the second ruffian, *Jubelo*, with more violence, and on his refusal to comply with his request, he gave him a severe blow with the square across his breast; on which he attempted to make his escape at the East gate, where he was accosted by the third ruffian, *Jubelum*, with still more violence, and on refusing to comply with his request, the ruffian gave him a violent blow with the common gavel, on the forehead, which brought him to the floor; on which one of them exclaimed, 'What shall we do; we have killed our Grand Master, Hiram Abbiff? another answers, 'Let's carry him out at the E. gate and bury him in the rubbish until low twelve, and then meet and carry him a Westerly course and bury him.' The Candidate is then taken up in a blanket, on which he fell, and carried to the W. end of the Lodge, and covered up and left; by this time the Master has resumed his seat (King Solomon is supposed to arrive at the Temple at this juncture), and calls to order, and asks the Senior Warden the cause of all that confusion; the Senior Warden answers, 'Our Grand Master, Hiram Abbiff, is missing, and there are no plans or designs laid down on the Trestle-board, for the crafts to pursue their labors.' The Master, alias King Solomon, replies, 'Our Grand Master missing? Our Grand Master has always been very punctual in his attendance; I fear he is indisposed; assemble the Crafts and search in and about the Temple, and see if he can be found.' They all shuffle about the floor awhile, when the master calls them to order, and asks the Senior Warden 'what success,' he answers, 'We cannot find our Grand Master, my lord.' The Master then orders the secretary to call the roll of workmen, and see whether any of them are missing. The secretary calls the roll, and says, 'I have called the roll, my lord, and find that there are three missing, viz: *Jubela, Jubelo* and *Jubelum*.' His lordship then observed; 'This brings to my mind a circumstance that took place this morning; twelve Fellow-Crafts, clothed in white gloves and aprons, in token of their innocence, came to me and confessed that they twelve, with three others, had conspired to extort the Master-Mason's word from their Grand Master, Hiram Abbiff; and in case of refusal, to take his life—they twelve had recanted, but feared the other three had been base enough to carry their atrocious designs into execution.' Solomon then ordered twelve Fellow-Crafts to be drawn from the bands of the workmen, clothed in white gloves and aprons, in token of their innocence, and sent three east, three west, three north and three south, in search of the ruffians, and if found, to bring them forward. Here the members all shuffle about the floor awhile, and fall in with a reputed traveler, and inquire of him if he had seen any traveling men that way; he tells them that he had seen three that morning near the coast of Joppa, who from their dress and appearance were Jews, and were workmen from the temple, inquiring for a passage to Ethiopia, but were unable to obtain one in consequence of an embargo which had recently been laid on all the shipping, and had turned back into the country.

The Master now calls them to order again, and asks the Senior Warden. 'what success;' he answers by relating what had taken place; Solomon observes, 'I had this embargo laid to prevent the ruffians from making their escape,' and adds, 'you will go and search again, and search until you find them, if possible, and if they are not found, the twelve who confessed, shall be considered as the reputed murderers, and suffer accordingly.' The members all start again and shuffle about awhile, until one of them, as if by accident, finds the body of Hiram Abbiff; alias the Candidate, and hails his traveling companions, who join him, and while they are humming out something over the Candidate, the three reputed ruffians, who are seated in a private corner near the Candidate, are heard to exclaim in the following manner; first, *Jubela*, 'O that my throat had been cut across, my tongue torn out, and my body buried in the rough sands of the sea at low watermark, where the tide ebbs and flows twice in twenty-four hours, ere I had been accessory to the death of so good a man as our Grand Master, Hiram Abbiff.'

The second, *Jubelo*, 'O that my left breast had been torn open, and my heart and vitals taken from thence and thrown over my left shoulder, carried into the valley of Jehosaphat, and there to become a prey to the wild beasts of the field and vultures of the air, ere I had conspired the death of so good a man as our Grand Master, Hiram Abbiff.'

The third, *Jubelum*, 'O that my body had been severed in two in the midst, and divided to the North and the South, my bowels burnt to ashes in the center, and the ashes scattered by the four winds of heaven, that there might not the least track or trace of remembrance remain among men, or Masons of so vile and perjured a wretch as I am—Ah, *Jubela* and *Jubelo*, it was I that struck him harder than you both; it was I that gave him the fatal blow; it was I that killed him outright.' The three Fellow-Crafts, who had stood by the Candidate all this time listening to the ruffians, whose voices they recognized, say one to the other, 'What shall we do, there are three of them, and only three of us;' 'it is,' said one, in reply, 'our cause is good, let us seize them;' on which they rush forward, seize and carry them to the Master, to whom they relate what had passed; the Master then addresses them in the following [they in many Lodges kneel, or lie down in token of their guilt and penitence.] 'Well Jubela, what have you got to say for yourself, guilty or not guilty?' *Ans.* 'Guilty my Lord.' 'Jubelo, guilty or not guilty?' *Ans.* 'Guilty my Lord.' 'Jubelum, guilty or not guilty? *Ans.* 'Guilty my Lord.' The Master to the three Fellow-Crafts who took them: 'Take them without the west gate of the Temple and have them executed according to the several imprecations of their own mouths.' They are then hurried off to the west end of the room. Here this part of the farce ends. The master then orders fifteen Fellow-Crafts to be selected from the bands of the workmen, and sent three East, three West, three North, three South, and three in and about the temple in search of their grand Master, Hiram Abbiff (in some Lodges they only send twelve, when their own lectures say fifteen, were sent) and charges them if they find the body to examine carefully on and about it for the master's word, or a key to it. The three that traveled a westerly course, come to the Candidate and finger about him a little and are called to order by the Master, when they report that they had found the grave of their grand Master, Hiram Abbiff, and on moving the earth until they come to the body, they involuntarily found their hands raised in this positon (showing it at the same time; it is the due-guard of this degree) to guard their nostrils against the offensive effluvia which arose from the grave, and that they had searched carefully on and about the body for the Master's word, but had not discovered anything but a faint resemblance of the letter G on the left breast. The Master, on the receipt of this information (raising himself), raises his hands three several times above his head, [as hereinbefore described], and exclaims, 'Nothing but a faint resemblance of the letter G! that is not the Master's word, nor a key to it. I fear the Master's word is forever lost! Nothing but a faint resemblance of the letter G! that is not the Master's word, nor a key to it. I fear the Master's word is forever lost!' [The third exclamation is different from the other two—attend to it, it has been described in page 59], 'Nothing but a faint resemblance of the letter G! that is not the Master's word, nor a key to it. O Lord, my God, is there no help for the widow's son!' The Master then orders the Junior Warden to summon a Lodge of Entered Apprentice Masons, and repair to the grave and try to raise the body of their Grand Master, by the Entered Apprentice's grip. They go to the Candidate and take hold of his fore-finger and pull it, return and tell the Master that they could not raise him by the Entered Apprentice's grip, that the skin cleaved from the bone. A Lodge of Fellow-Crafts are then sent, who act as before, except they pull the Candidate's second finger. The Master then directs the Senior Warden [generally] to summon a Lodge of Master-Masons and says, 'I will go with them myself in person, and try to raise the body by the Master's grip, or lion's paw.' [Some say by the strong grip or lion's paw]. They then all assemble round the Candidate, the Master having declared that the first word spoken after the body was raised, should be adopted as a substitute for the Master's word, for the government of Master-Mason's Lodges in all future generations; he proceeds to raise the Candidate, alias the representative of the dead body of Hiram Abbiff. He [the Candidate], is raised on what is called the five points of fellowship, which are foot to foot, knee to knee, breast to breast, hand to back, and mouth to ear. This is done by putting the inside of your right foot to the inside of the right foot of the person to whom you are going to give the word, the inside of your knee to his, laying your right breast against his, your left hands on the back of each other, and your mouths to each other's right ear [in which position alone you are permitted to give the word], and whisper the word *Mah-hah-bone*. The Master's grip is given by taking hold of each other's right hand as though you were going to shake hands, and sticking the nails of each of your fingers into the joint of the other's wrist where it unites with the hand. In this position the Candidate is raised, he keeping his whole body stiff, as though dead. The Master in raising him is assisted by some of the brethren, who take hold of the Candidate by the arms and shoulders; as soon as he is raised to his feet, they step back, and the Master whispers the word *Mah-hah-bone* in his ear and causes the Candidate to repeat it, telling him at the same time that he must never give it in any manner other than that which he receives it.—He is also told that *Mah-hah-bone* signifies marrow in the bone.—They then separate, and the Master makes the following explanation respecting the five points of fellowship.—Master to Candidate, 'Brother, foot to foot, teaches you that you should whenever asked, go on a brother's errand if within the length of your Cable-Tow, even if you should have to go barefoot and barehead. Knee to knee, that you should always remember a Master-Mason in your devotion to Almighty God. Breast to breast, that you should keep the Master-Mason's secrets, when given to you in charge as such, as secure and inviolable in your breast, as they were in his own before communicated to you. Hand to back, that you should support a Master-Mason behind his back as well as before his face. Mouth to ear, that you should support his good name as well behind his back as before his face.' After the Candidate is through what is called the work part, the Master addresses him in the folfowing manner; Brother, you may suppose from the manner you have been dealt with to-night, that we have been fooling with you, or that we have treated you differently from others, but I assure you that is not the case. You have this night represented one of the greatest men that ever lived, in the tragical catastrophe of his death, burial and resurrection; I mean Hiram Abbiff, the widow's son, who was slain by three ruffians at the building of King Solomon's Temple, and who in his inflexibility, integrity and fortitude, never was surpassed by man. The history of that momentous event is thus related. Masonic tradition informs us that at the building of King Solomons Temple, fifteen Fellow-Crafts discovered that the Temple was almost finished, and not having the Master-Mason's word, became very impatient, and entered into a horrid conspiracy to extort the Master-Mason's word from their Grand Master, Hiram Abbiff, the first time they met him alone, or take his life, that they might pass as Masters in other countries and receive wages as such; but before they could accomplish their designs, twelve of them recanted, but the other three were base enough to carry their atrocious designs into execution. Their names were *Jubela, Jubelo* and *Jubelum*.

'It was the custom of our Grand Master, Hiram Abbiff, every day at high twelve, when the Crafts were from labor to refreshment, to enter into the *sanctum sanctorum* and offer up his devotions to the ever living God, and draw out his plans and designs on his Trestle-board for the Crafts to pursue their labor. On a certain day (not named in any of the traditional accounts), *Jubela, Jubelo,* and *Jubelum,* placed themselves at the south, west, and east gates of the Temple. And Hiram having finished his devotions and labor, attempted (as was his usual custom) to retire at the south gate, where he was met by *Jubela,* who demanded of him the Master-Mason's word (some say the secrets of a Master-Mason), and on his refusal to give it, *Jubela* gives him a violent blow with the twenty-four inch gauge across the throat; on which Hiram fled to the west gate, where he was accosted in the same manner by *Jubelo,* but with more violence.—Hiram told him that he could not give the word then, because Solomon, King of Israel, Hiram, King of Tyre, and himself, had entered into a solemn league, that the word never should be given unless they three were present, but if he would wait with patience, until the Grand Lodge assembled at Jerusalem, if he was then found worthy he should receive it, otherwise he could not; *Jubelo* replied in a very peremptory manner; 'If you do not give me the Master's word, I'll take your life;' and on Hiram's refusing to give it, Jubelo gave him a severe blow with the square across the left breast, on which he fled to the east gate, where he was accosted by *Jubelum* in the same manner, but with still more violence. Here Hiram reasoned as before; Jubelum told him that he had heard his caviling with Jubela and Jubelo long enough, and that the Master's word had been promised to him from time to time, for a long time, that he was still put off and the temple was almost finished, and he was determined to have the word or take his life; 'I want it so that I may be able to get wages as a Master-Mason in any country to which I may go for employment, after the Temple is finished, and that I may be able to support my wife and children.' Hiram, persisting in his refusal; Jubelum gave him a violent blow with the gavel on the forehead, which felled him to the floor and killed him:—they took the body and carried it out of the west gate and buried it in the rubbish until low twelve at night (which is twelve o'clock), when they three met agreeably to appointment, and carried the body a westerly course and buried it at the brow of a hill in a grave dug due east and west, six feet perpendicular, and made their escape. King Solomon coming up to the Temple at low six in the morning (as was his ususal custom), found the Crafts all in confusion; and on inquiring the cause, was informed that their Grand Master, Hiram Abbiff was missing, and there were no plans and designs laid down on the Trestle-board for the Crafts to pursue their labor. Solomon ordered immediate search to be made in and about the Temple for him; no discovery being made, he then ordered the Secretary to call the roll of workmen to see if any were missing; it appearing that there were three, viz: *Jubela, Jubelo,* and *Jubelum;* Solomon observed, 'This brings to my mind a circumstance that took place this morning. Twelve Fellow-Crafts came to me dressed in white gloves and aprons in token of their innocence, and confessed that they twelve, with three others, had conspired to extort the Master-Mason's word from their Grand Master, Hiram Abbiff, and in case of his refusal to take his life; they twelve had recanted, but feared the other three had been base enough to carry their atrocious design into execution.' Solomon immediately ordered twelve Fellow-Crafts to be selected from the bands of the workmen, clothed in white gloves and aprons in token of their innocence, and sent three East, three West, three North, and three South, in search of the ruffians, and if found to bring them up before him.—The three that traveled a westerly course, coming near the coast of Joppa, fell in with a wayfaring man, who informed them that he had seen three men pass that way that morning, who, from their appearance and dress, were workmen from the Temple, inquiring for a passage to Ethiopia, but were unable to obtain one in consequence of an embargo which had recently been laid on all the shipping, and had turned back into the country. After making still further and more diligent search, and making no further discovery, they returned to the Temple and reported to Solomon the result of their pursuit and inquiries. On which Solomon directed them to go and search again, and search until they found their Grand Master, Hiram Abbiff, if possible, and if he was not found, the twelve who had confessed, should be considered as the murderers and suffer accordingly.

They returned again in pursuit of the ruffians, and one of the three that traveled a westerly course, being more weary than the rest, sat down at the brow of a hill to rest and refresh himself; and, in attempting to rise, caught hold of a sprig of cassia, which easily gave way, and excited his curiosity, and made him suspicious of a deception, on which he hailed his companions, who immediately assembled, and, on examination, found that the earth had been recently moved; and on moving the rubbish, discovered the appearance of a grave; and while they were confabulating about what measures to take, they heard voices issuing from a cavern in the clefts of the rocks, on which, they immediately repaired to the place, where they heard the voice of *Jubela* exclaim, 'O! that my throat had been cut across, and my tongue torn out, and my body buried in the rough sands of the sea at low water-mark, where the tide ebbs and flows twice in twenty-four hours, ere I had been accessory to the death of so good a man as our Grand Master, Hiram Abbiff'—on which, they distinctly heard the voice of *Jubelo* exclaim, 'O! that my breast had been torn open, and my heart and vitals taken from thence and thrown over my left shoulder, to the valley of Jehosaphat, there to become a prey to the wild beasts of the field and vultures of the air, ere I had conspired to take the life of so good a man as our Grand Master, Hiram Abbiff'—when they more distinctly heard the voice of *Jubelum* exclaim, 'O! that my body had been severed in two in the midst, and divided to the north and the south, my bowels burnt to ashes in the center, and the ashes scattered by the four winds of heaven, that there might not remain the least track or trace of remembrance among men or Masons of so vile and perjured a wretch as I am, who willfully took the life of so good a man as our Grand Master, Hiram Abbiff. Ah! *Jubela* and *Jubelo*, it was I that struck him harder than you both! it was I that gave him the fatal blow! it was I that killed him outright!' On which, they rushed forward, seized, bound, and carried them up before King Solomon, who, after hearing the testimony of the three Fellow-Crafts, and the three ruffians having plead guilty, ordered them to be taken out at the west gate of the Temple and executed agreeable to the several imprecations of their own mouths. King Solomon then ordered fifteen Fellow-Crafts to be selected from the bands of the workmen, clothed with white gloves and aprons, in token of their innocence, and sent three East, three West, three North, three South, and three in and about the Temple, in search of the their Grand Master, Hiram Abbiff; and the three that traveled a westerly course found it under that sprig of Cassia where a worthy Brother sat down to rest and refresh himself; and on removing the earth until they came to the coffin, they involuntarily found their hands raised, as hereinbefore described, to guard their nostrils against the offensive effluvia that arose from the grave. It is also said that the body had laid there fourteen days, some say fifteen. The body was raised in the manner hereinbefore described, carried up to the Temple, and buried as explained in the closing clauses of the lecture. Not one-third part of the preceding history of this degree is ever given to a Candidate. A few general desultory, unconnected remarks are made to him, and he is generally referred to the manner of raising, and the lecture, for information as to the particulars. Here follows a charge which ought to be, and sometimes is, delivered to the Candidate after hearing the history of the degree.

AN ADDRESS TO BE DELIVERED TO THE CANDIDATE AFTER THE HISTORY HAS BEEN GIVEN.

'Brother, your zeal for the institution of Masonry, the progress you have made in the mystery, and your conformity to our regulations, have pointed you out as a proper object of our favor and esteem.

'You are bound by duty, honor, and gratitude, to be faithful to your trust; to support the dignity of your character on every occasion: and to enforce, by precept and example, obedience to the tenets of the Order.

'In the character of a Master-Mason, you are authorized to correct the errors and irregularities of your uninformed Brethren, and to guard them against a breach of fidelity.

'To preserve the reputation of the Fraternity unsullied, must be your constant care; and for this purpose it is your province to recommend to your inferiors, obedience and submission; to your equals, courtesy, and affability; to your superiors, kindness and condescension. Universal benevolence you are always to inculcate; and, by the regularity of your own behavior, afford the best example for the conduct of others less informed. The ancient landmarks of the Order, intrusted to your care, you are carefully to preserve; and never suffer them to be infringed, or countenance a deviation from the established usages and customs of the fraternity.

'Your virtue, honor, and reputation are concerned in supporting with dignity the character you now bear. Let no motive, therefore, make you swerve from your duty, violate your vows, or betray your trust; but be true and faithful, and imitate the example of that celebrated artist whom you this evening represent; thus you will render yourself deserving the honor which we have conferred, and merit the confidence that we have reposed.'

Here follows the lecture on this degree, which is divided into three sections.

SECTION FIRST.

Q. Are you a Master-Mason?

A. I am—try me, prove me—disprove me, if you can.

Q. Where was you prepared to be made a Master-Mason?

A. In a room adjacent to the body of a just and lawfully constituted Lodge of such, duly assembled in a room, representing the sanctum sanctorum, or holy of holies, of King Solomon's Temple.

Q. How was you prepared?

A. By being divested of all metals; neither naked nor clothed; barefoot nor shod; with a Cable-Tow three times about my naked body; in which posture I was conducted to the door of the Lodge, where I gave three distinct knocks.

Q. What did those three distinct knocks allude to?

A. To the third degree of Masonry; it being that on which I was about to enter.

Q. What was said to you from within?

A. Who comes there? who comes there? who comes there?

Q. Your answer?

A. A worthy Brother, who has been regularly initiated as an Entered Apprentice Mason, passed to the degrees of a Fellow-Craft, and now wishes for further light in Masonry by being raised to the sublime degree of a Master-Mason.

Q. What further was said to you from within?

A. I was asked if it was of my own free will and accord I made that request; if I was duly and truly prepared; worthy and well qualified, and had made suitable proficiency in the preceding degrees; all of which being answered in the affirmative, I was asked by what further rights I expected to obtain that benefit.

Q. Your answer?

A. By the benefit of a pass-word.

Q. What is the pass-word?

A. *Tubal Cain.*

Q. What next was said to you?

A. I was bid to wait until the Worshipful Master in the East was made acquainted with my request, and his answer returned.

Q. What followed after his answer was returned?

A. I was caused to enter the Lodge on the two extreme points of the compass, pressing my naked right and left breasts, in the name of the Lord.

Q. How was you then disposed of?

A. I was conducted three times regularly round the Lodge, and halted at the Junior Warden in the South, where the same questions were asked and answers returned as at the door.

Q. How did the Junior Warden dispose of you?

A. He ordered me to be conducted to the Senior Warden in the West where the same questions were asked and answers returned as before.

Q. How did the Senior Warden dispose of you?

A. He ordered me to be conducted to the Worshipful Master in the East, where, by him, the same questions were asked and answers returned as before, who likewise demanded of me, from whence I came, and whither I was traveling.

Q. Your answer?

A. From the East and traveling to the West

Q. Why do you leave the East and travel to the West

A. In search of light.

E

Q. How did the Worshipful Master then dispose of you?

A. He ordered me to be conducted back to the West, from whence I came, and put in care of the Senior Warden, who taught me how to approach the East, by advancing upon three upright regular steps to the third step, my feet forming a square, and my body erect at the altar before the Worshipful Master.

Q. What did the Worshipful Master do with you?

A. He made an obligated Master-Mason of me.

Q. How?   A. In due form.

Q. What was that due form?

A. Both my knees bare bent, they forming a square; both hands on the Holy Bible, square, and compass; in which posture I took upon me the solemn oath or obligation of a Master-Mason.

Q. After your obligation, what was said to you?

A. What do you most desire?

Q. Your answer?

A. More light. [The bandage round the head is now dropped over the eyes.]

Q. Did you receive light?   A. I did.

Q. On being brought to light on this degree, what did you first discover?

A. Three great lights in Masonry, by the assistance of three less, and both points of the compass elevated above the square, which denoted to me that I had received, or was about to receive all the light that could be conferred on me in a Master's Lodge.

Q. What did you next discover?

A. The Worshipful Master approaching me from the east under the sign and due-guard of a Master-Mason, who presented me with his right-hand in token of Brotherly love, and confidence, and proceeded to give me the pass-grip and word of a Master-Mason [the word is the name of the pass-grip], and bid me rise and salute the Junior and Senior Wardens, and convince them that I was an obligated Master-Mason, and had the sign, pass-grip and word. [Tubal-Cain.]

Q. What did you next discover?

A. The Worshipful Master approaching me a second time from the east, who presented me with a lamb-skin or white apron, which he said he hoped I would continue to wear with honor to myself, and satisfaction and advantage to the Brethren.

Q. What was you next presented with?

A. The working tools of a Master-Mason.

Q. What are they?

A. All the implements of Masonry indiscriminately, but more especially the trowel

Q. How explained?

A. The trowel is an instrument made use of by operative Masons to spread the cement which unites a building into one common mass, but we, as free and accepted Masons, are taught to make use of it for the more noble and glorious purpose, of spreading the cement of Brotherly love and affection; that cement which unites us into one sacred band or society of Brothers, among whom no contention should ever exist, but that noble emulation, of who can best work or best agree.

Q. What was you next presented with?

A. Three precious jewels.

Q. What are they?

A. Humanity, Friendship, and Brotherly love.

Q. How was you then disposed of?

A. I was conducted out of the Lodge and invested with what I had been divested, and returned again in due season.

SECTION SECOND.

Q. Did you ever return to the sanctum sanctorum or holy of holies of King Solomon's Temple?

A. I did.

Q. Was there anything particular took place on your return?

A. There was, viz: I was accosted by three ruffians, who demanded of me the Master-Mason's word.

Q. Did you give it to them?

A. I did not, but bid them wait with time and patience until the Grand Lodge assembled at Jerusalem; and then, if they were found worthy, they should receive it; otherwise they could not.

Q. In what manner was you accosted?

A. In attempting to retire at the South gate, I was accosted by one of them, who demanded of me the Master-Mason's word, and on my refusing to comply with his request, he gave me a blow with the twenty-four inch gauge across my breast, on which I fled to the West-gate, where I was accosted by the second with more violence, and on my refusing to comply with his request, he gave me a severe blow with the square across my breast, on which I attempted to make my escape at the east gate, where I was accosted by the third with still more violence, and on my refusing to comply with his request, he gave me a violent blow with the common gavel, on the forehead, and brought me to the floor.

Q. Whom did you represent at that time?

A. Our Grand Master, Hiram Abbiff, who was slain at the building of King Solomon's Temple.

Q. Was his death premeditated?

A. It was, by fifteen Fellow-Crafts, who conspired to extort the Master Mason's word; twelve of whom recanted, but the other three were base enough to carry their atrocious designs into execution.

Q. What did they do with the body?

A. They carried it out at the West gate of the Temple and buried it until low twelve at night, when they three met agreeably to appointment, and carried it a westerly course from the Temple, and buried it under the brow of a hill in a grave six feet due east and west, six feet perpendicular, and made their escape.

Q. What time was he slain?

A. At high twelve at noon, when the Crafts were from labor to refreshment.

Q. How came he to be alone at that time?

A. Because it was the usual custom of our Grand Master, Hiram Abbiff, every day at high twelve, when the Crafts were from labor to refreshment, to enter into the sanctum sanctorum or holy of holies, and offer up his adorations to the ever living God, and draw out his plans and designs on his Trestle-board for the Crafts to pursue their labor.

Q. At what time was he missing?

A. At low six in the morning, when King Solomon came up to the Temple as usual to view the work, and found the Crafts all in confusion, and on inquiring the cause, he was informed that their Grand Master, Hiram Abbiff was missing, and no plans or designs were laid down on the Trestle-board for the Crafts to pursue their labor.

Q. What observations did King Solomon make at that time?

A. He observed that our Grand Master, Hiram Abbiff had always been very punctual in attending, and feared that he was indisposed, and ordered search to be made in and about the Temple, to see if he could be found.

Q. Search being made, and he not found, what further remarks did King Solomon make?

A. He observed, he feared some fatal accident had befallen our Grand Master, Hiram Abbiff; that morning, twelve Fellow-Crafts, clothed in white gloves and aprons in token of their innocence, had confessed that they twelve, with three others, had conspired to extort the Master-Mason's word from their Grand Master, Hiram Abbiff, or take his Life; that they twelve had recanted, but feared the other three had been base enough to carry their atrocious designs into execution.

Q. What followed?

A. King Solomon ordered the roll of workmen to be called to see if there were any missing.

Q. The roll being called, were there any missing?

A. There were three, viz: Jubela, Jubelo, and Jubelum.

Q. Were the ruffians ever found?

A. They were.

Q. How?

A. By the wisdom of King Solomon, who ordered twelve Fellow-Crafts to be selected from the bands of the workmen, clothed in white gloves and aprons, in token of their innocence, and sent three east, three west, three north, and three south in search of the ruffians, and if found to bring them forward.

Q. What success?

A. The three that traveled a westerly course from the Temple, coming near the coast of Joppa, were informed by a wayfaring man, that three men had been seen that way that morning, who from their appearance and dress were workmen from the Temple, inquiring for a passage to Ethiopia, but were unable to obtain one in consequence of an embargo which had recently been laid on all the shipping, and had turned back into the country.

Q. What followed?

A. King Solomon ordered them to go and search again, and search until they were found, if possible, and if they were not found, that the twelve who had confessed should be considered as the reputed murderers, and suffer accordingly.

Q. What success?

A. One of the three that traveled a westerly course from the Temple, being more weary than the rest, sat down under the brow of a hill to rest and refresh himself, and in attempting to rise, caught hold of a sprig of cassia, which easily gave way, and excited his curiosity and made him suspicious of a deception, on which he hailed his companions, who immediately assembled, and on examination, found that the earth had recently been moved, and on moving the rubbish discovered the appearance of a grave; and while they were confabulating about what measures to take, they heard voices issuing from a cavern in the clefts of the rocks; on which they immediately repaired to the place, where they heard the voice of Jubela exclaim, 'O, that my throat had been cut across, my tongue torn out, and my body buried in the rough sands of the sea at low water-mark, where the tide ebbs and flows twice in twenty-four hours, ere I had been accessory to the death of so good a man as our Grand Master, Hiram Abbiff!' On which they distinctly heard the voice of Jubelo exclaim, 'O, that my left breast had been torn open, and my heart and vitals taken from thence, thrown over my left shoulder, carried to the valley of Jehosaphat, there to become a prey to the wild beasts of the field and vultures of the air, ere I had conspired to take the life of so good a man as our Grand Master, Hiram Abbiff!' when they more distinctly heard the voice of Jubelum exclaim, 'O, that my body had been severed in two in the midst, and divided to the North and the South, and my bowels burnt to ashes in the center, and the ashes scattered before (or by) the four winds of heaven that there might not remain the least track or trace of remembrance among men or Masons of so vile and perjured a wretch as I am, who willfully took the life of so good a man as our Grand Master, Hiram Abbiff! Ah, Jubela and Jubelo, it was I that struck him harder than you both, it was I that gave him the fatal blow, it was I that killed him outright.' On which they rushed forward, seized, bound and carried them up to the Temple to King Solomon.

Q. What did King Solomon do with them?
A. He ordered them to be executed agreeably to the several imprecations of their own mouths.

Q. Was the body of our Grand Master, Hiram Abbiff, ever found?
A. It was. Q. How?
A. By the wisdom of King Solomon, who ordered fifteen (in some Lodges they say twelve) Fellow-Crafts to be selected from the bands of the workmen, and sent three East, three West, three North, three South, and three in and about the Temple to search for the body.

Q. Where was it found?
A. Under that sprig of cassia where a worthy Brother sat down to rest and refresh himself.

Q. Was there anything particular took place on the discovery of the body?
A. There was, viz: on moving the earth until we came to the coffin, we involuntarily found our hands in this position, to guard our nostrils against the offensive effluvia which arose from the grave.

Q. How long had the body lain there?
A. Fourteen days.

Q. What did they do with the body?
A. Raised it in a Masonic form and carried it up to the Temple for more decent interment.

Q. Where was it buried?
A. Under the sanctum sanctorum, or holy of holies of King Solomon's Temple, over which they erected a marble monument with this inscription delineated thereon. A virgin weeping over a broken column, with a book open before her, in her right-hand a sprig of Cassia, in her left an urn, Time standing behind her with his hands infolded in the ringlets of her hair.

Q. What do they denote?
A. The weeping virgin denotes the unfinished state of the Temple; the broken column, that one of the principal supports of Masonry had fallen, the book open before her, that his memory, was on perpetual record; the sprig of cassia, the timely discovery of his grave; the urn in her left-hand, that his ashes are safely deposited under the sanctum sanctorum or holy of holies of King Solomon's Temple, and Time, standing behind her with his hands

infolded in the ringlets of her hair, that time, patience, and perseverance, will accomplish all things.

SECTION THIRD.

Q. What does a Master's Lodge represent?
A. The sanctum sanctorum or holy of holies of King Solomon's Temple.
Q. How long was the Temple building?
A. Seven years, during which it rained not in the day-time that the workmen might not be obstructed in their labor.
Q. What supported the Temple?
A. Fourteen hundred and fifty-three columns, and two thousand nine hundred and six pilasters; all hewn from the finest Parian marble.
Q. What farther supported it?
A. Three grand columns, or pillars
Q. What are they called?
A. Wisdom, Strength, and Beauty,
Q. What did they represent?
A. The pillar of Wisdom represented Solomon, King of Israel, whose wisdom contrived the mighty fabric; the pillar of Strength, Hiram, King of Tyre, who strengthened Solomon in his glorious undertaking; the pillar of beauty, Hiram Abbiff, the widow's son, whose cunning craft, and curious workmanship beautified and adorned the Temple.
Q. How many were there employed in the building of King Solomon's Temple?
A. Three Grand Masters, three thousand three hundred Masters, or overseers of the work, eighty thousand Fellow-Crafts, and seventy thousand Entered Apprentices; all these were classed and arranged in such a manner by the wisdom of Solomon, that neither envy, discord, nor confusion, were suffered to interrupt that universal peace and tranquillity that pervaded the work at that important period.
Q. How many constitute an Entered Apprentice Lodge?
A. Seven; one Master, and six Entered Apprentices.
Q. Where did they usually meet?
A. On the ground-floor of King Solomon's Temple.
Q. How many constitute a Fellow-Craft's Lodge?
A. Five; two Masters, and three Fellow-Crafts.
Q. Where did they usually meet?
A. In the middle-chamber of King Solomon's **Temple.**
Q. How many constitute a Master's Lodge?
A. Three Master-Masons.
Q. Where did they usually meet?

A. In the sanctum sanctorum or holy of holies of King Solomon's Temple.

Q. Have you any emblems on this degree?

Q. What are the first class?

A. The pot of incense; the bee-hive; the book of constitutions, guarded by the Tyler's sword ; the sword pointing to a naked heart; the all-seeing eye; the anchor and ark; the forty-seventh problem of Euclid; the hour-glass; the scythe; and the three steps usually delineated on the Master's Carpet, which are thus explained:—The pot of *incense* is an emblem of a pure heart which is always an acceptable sacrifice to the deity; and as this glows with fervent heat, so should our hearts continually glow with gratitude to the great and beneficent Author of our existence, for the manifold blessings and comforts we enjoy.—The *bee-hive*, is an emblem of industry, and recommends the practice of that virtue to all created beings, from the highest seraph in heaven to the lowest reptile of the dust. It teaches us that, as we came into the world rational intelligent beings, so we should ever be industrious ones; never sitting down contented while our fellow creatures around us are in want; when it is in our power to relieve them, without inconvenience to ourselves. When we take a survey of nature, we behold man, in his infancy, more helpless and indigent than the brute creation: he lies languishing for days, weeks, months, and years, totally incapable of providing sustenance for himself; of guarding against the attacks of the wild beasts of the field, or sheltering himself from the inclemencies of the weather. It might have pleased the great Creator of heaven and earth to have made man independent of all other beings; but, as dependence is one of the strongest bonds of society, mankind were made dependent on each other for protection and security, as they thereby enjoy better opportunities of fulfilling the duties of reciprocal love and friendship. Thus was man formed for social and active life, the noblest part of the work of God; and he that will so demean himself as not to be endeavoring to add to the common stock of knowledge and understanding, may be deemed a *drone* in the *hive* of nature—a useless member of society, and unworthy of our protection as Masons:—The *Book of Constitutions, guarded by the Tyler's sword*, reminds us that we should be ever watchful and guarded, in our thoughts, words and actions, particularly when before the enemies of Masonry ; ever bearing in remembrance those truly Masonic virtues, *silence* and *circumspection*.—The *sword pointing to a naked heart*, demonstrates that justice will sooner or later overtake us; and although our thoughts, words, and actions may be hidden from the eyes of man; yet that *all-seeing eye*, whom the *sun, moon*, and *stars* obey, and under whose watchful care even comets perform their stupendous revolutions, pervades the inmost recesses of the human heart, and will reward us according to our merits.—The *anchor* and *ark*, are emblems of a well-grounded *hope*, and a well-spent life They are emblematical of that divine *ark* which safely wafts us over this tempestuous sea of troubles, and that *anchor* which shall safely moor us in a peaceful harbor, where the wicked cease from troubling, and the weary shall find rest. The *forty-seventh problem of Euclid.* This was an invention of our ancient friend and Brother, the great Pythagoras, who in his travels through Asia, Africa, and Europe, was initiated into several orders of priesthood, and raised to the sublime degree of a Master-Mason. This wise philosopher enriched his mind abundantly in a general knowledge of things, and more especially in geometry, or masonry: on this subject he drew out many problems and theorems; and among the most distinguished he erected this, which, in the joy of his heart, he called *Eureka*, in the Grecian language signifying, *I have found it;* and upon the discovery of which he is said to have discovered a hecatomb. It teaches Masons to be general lovers of the arts and sciences. The *hour-glass* is an emblem of human life. Behold! how swiftly the sands run, and how rapidly our lives are drawing to a close. We cannot without astonishment behold the little particles which are contained in this machine; how they pass away almost imperceptibly, and yet, to our surprise, in the short space of an hour they are all exhausted. Thus wastes man! to day he puts forth the tender leaves of hope; to-morrow, blossoms, and bears his blushing honors thick upon him; the next day comes a frost which nips the shoot, and when he thinks his greatness is still ripening, he falls, like autumn leaves, to enrich our mother earth.—The *scythe* is an emblem of time, which cuts the brittle thread of life, and launches us into eternity. Behold! what havoc the scythe of time makes among the human race; if by chance we should escape the numerous evils incident to childhood and youth, and with health and vigor arrive to the years of manhood, yet with all we must soon be cut down by the all-devouring scythe of time, and be gathered into the land where our fathers have gone before us.—The *three steps* usually delineated upon the Master's carpet, are emblematical of the three principal stages of human life, viz: youth, manhood, and age. In youth, as Entered Apprentices, we ought industriously to occupy our minds in the attainment of useful knowledge: in manhood, as Fellow-Crafts, we should apply our knowledge to the discharge of our respective duties to God, our neighbors, and ourselves; that so in age, as Master-Masons we may enjoy the happy reflections consequent on a well-spent life, and die in the hope of a glorious immortality.

Q. What are the second class of emblems?

A. The spade, coffin, death-head, marrow bones, and sprig of cassia, which are thus explained: The *spade* opens the vault to receive our bodies, where our active limbs will soon molder to dust.—The *coffin, death-head,* and *marrow-bones,* are emblematical of the death and burial of our Grand Master, Hiram Abbiff, and are worthy of our serious attention. The *sprig of cassia* is emblematical of that immortal part of man which never dies—

and when the cold winter of death shall have passed, and the bright summer's morn of the resurrection appears, the Sun of Righteousness shall descend, and send forth his angels to collect our ransomed dust; then, if we are found worthy, by his pass-word, we shall enter into the celestial Lodge above, where the Supreme Architect of the Universe presides, where we shall see the King in the beauty of holiness, and with him enter into an endless eternity.

Here end the three first degrees of Masonry, which constitute a Master-Mason's Lodge. A Master-Mason's Lodge and a Chapter of Royal Arch Masons, are two distinct bodies, wholly independent of each other. The members of a Chapter are privileged to visit all Master-Masons' Lodges when they please, and may be, and often are, members of both at the same time; and all the members of a Master-Mason's Lodge who are Royal Arch Masons, though not members of any Chapter, may visit any Chapter. I wish the reader to understand that neither all Royal Arch Masons nor Master-Masons are members of either Lodge or Chapter: there are tens of thousands who are not members, and scarcely ever attend although privileged to do so.

A very small proportion of Masons, comparatively speaking, ever advance any further than the third degree, and consequently never get the great word which was lost by Hiram's untimely death. Solomon, king of Israel, Hiram, king of Tyre, and Hiram Abbiff, the widow's son, having sworn that they, nor neither of them would ever give the word except they three were present [and it is generally believed that there was not another person in the world at that time that had it]; consequently, the word was lost, and supposed to be forever; but the sequel will show it was found, after a lapse of four hundred and seventy years, notwithstanding the word *Mah-hah-bon*, which was substituted by Solomon, still continues to be used by Master-Masons, and no doubt will as long as Masonry attracts the attention of men; and the word which was lost is used in the Royal Arch degree. What was the word of the Royal Arch degree before they found the Master's word, which was lost at the death of Hiram Abbiff, and was not found for four hundred and seventy years? Were there any Royal Arch Masons before the Master's word was found?—I wish some Masonic gentleman would solve these two questions.

The ceremonies, history, and the lecture, in the preceding degree, are so similar, that, perhaps, some one of the three might have been dispensed with, and the subject well understood by most readers; notwithstanding, there is a small difference between the work and history, and between the history and the lecture.

I shall now proceed with the Mark-Master's degree, which is the first degree in the Chapter. The Mark-Master's degree, the Past-Master's, and the Most Excellent Masters' are called Lodges of Mark-Master Masons,

Past-Masters, and Most Excellent Masters; yet, although called Lodges, they are a component part of the Chapter. Ask a Mark-Master Mason if he belongs to the Chapter, he will tell you he does, but that he has only been marked. It is not an uncommon thing, by any means, for a Chapter to confer all four of the degrees in one night, viz: the Mark-Master, Past-Master, Most Excellent Master, and Royal Arch Degrees

---

THE FOLLOWING ARE THE SIGNS, DUE-GARDS, GRIPS, PASS-GRIPS, WORDS, AND PASS-WORDS OF THE THREE PRECEDING DEGREES.

ENTERED APPRENTICE'S DEGREE.

Sign.—Hold the two hands transversely across each other, the right-hand upward and one inch from the left.

Due-Guard.—Draw the right-hand across the throat, the thumb next to the throat, the arm as high as the elbow in the horizontal position, and let the hand fall down by the side.

Grip.—The right-hands are joined together, as in shaking hands, and each sticks his thumb-nail into the third joint or upper end of the fore-finger.

Word.—BO-AZ, which is given by lettering or halving.

FELLOW-CRAFT'S DEGREE.

Sign.—Draw your right hand flat, with the palm of it next to your breast, across the breast, from left to right, with some quickness, as if you were going to tear open the left breast, and let it drop down by your side.

Due-Guard.—Raise the left arm until that part of it between the elbow and the shoulder is perfectly horizontal, and raising the rest of the arm in a vertical position, so that that part of the arm below the elbow, and that part above it, form a square. The sign and due-guard are given at the same time in this degree.

Pass-grip.—Take each other by the right hand, as if to shake hands, and each put his thumb between the fore and second fingers, where they join the hand, and pressing the thumb between the joints. The name of the pass-grip is *Shibboleth*, and is the pass-word.

Real-grip.—Take each other by the right hand, as if to shake hands, and put the thumb on the joint of the second finger where it joins the hand, and crooking the thumb so that each can stick the nail of his thumb into the joint of the other.

Word.—JA-CHIN—given in the same manner as in the first degree

MASTER-MASON'S DEGREE.

Sign.—Raise both hands and arms perpendicularly, one on either side of the head, the elbow forming a square. The words accompanying this sign, in case of distress, are, " *O Lord my God, is there no help for the widow's son?* " As the last words are pronounced let the hands fall with an air of solemnity.—These words cannot be given except in the dark, when the sign cannot be seen, and is the sign of distress in this degree.

Due-guard.—Put the right-hand to the left side of the bowels, the hand open, with the thumb next to the belly, and let it fall: this is done tolerably quick.

Pass-grip.—Press the thumb between the joints of the second and third fingers where they join the hand. The name of it is *Tubal-Cain*, and is the pass-word.

Real-grip.—Take hold of each other's right hand, as if to shake hands, and stick the nails of each of your fingers into the joint of the other's wrist, where it unites with the hand.

Word.—MAH-HAH-BON. The word must be given in the following manner:—Place the inside of the right foot to the inside of the right foot of the person to whom you are going to give the word; the inside of your knee to his; laying your right breast against his; your left hands on each other's back, and your mouths to each other's right ear, when the word must be given not above a whisper. This word is sometimes vulgarly pronounced *Mah-mah-bo.*

A more full explanation of the signs, grips, words, &c., will be given at the conclusion of the second part of this work, which will comprise the following degrees, viz: Mark-Master, Present or Past-Master, Most Excellent Master, and the Royal Arch—to which will also be added, several of the degrees in the Order of Knighthood.

NOTE.—The publisher thinks proper to state, that as there has been much excitement on the appearance of this book, and various opinions as to the truth of the same, that the author of it was kidnapped and carried away from Batavia, by members of the Fraternity, to parts unknown, since which time he has not been heard from—and that at the late session of the Court of Oyer and Terminer, held at Canandaigua, Ontario Co., N. Y., on the 1st January, 1827, Loton Lawson, Nicholas G. Cheesbro, Edward Sawyer and John Sheldon, were arraigned for conspiring to do the same—the three first plead GUILTY to the charge, and Sheldon was tried and found GUILTY. They are now enduring their punishment, which was imprisonment in the common Jail of the county, for the following terms:—

Loton Lawson, 2 years, Nicholas G. Cheesbro, 1 year, John Sheldon, 3 months, Edward Sawyer, 1 month.

THE

SECOND PART:

OR

A KEY

TO THE HIGHER DEGREES

OF

FREEMASONRY:

GIVING A CLEAR AND CORRECT VIEW OF THE WAY AND MANNER OF CONFERRING THE DEGREES OF MARK-MASTER PAST-MASTER, MOST EXCELLENT MASTER AND ROYAL ARCH MASON, ON A CANDIDATE; AS PRACTICED IN ALL WELL-GOVERNED LODGES AND CHAPTERS THROUGHOUT THE GLOBE: TOGETHER WITH THE MEANS TO BE USED BY SUCH AS ARE NOT MASONS TO GAIN ADMISSION THEREIN — THE WHOLE INTENDED AS A GUIDE TO THE CRAFT AND A LIGHT TO THE UNENLIGHTENED

BY A MEMBER OF THE CRAFT.

"Put off thy shoes from off thy feet, for the place whereon thou standest is holy ground."—Exodus iii.

CINCINNATI.
PUBLISHED BY MATTHEW GARDINER.
::::::::

DISTRICT OF OHIO, TO WIT:

                        BE IT REMEMBERED, that on the ninth day of July, in the year of our Lord one thousand eight hundred and twenty-seven, [L.S.] and in the fifty-second year of American Independence, LEVI SMITH, of the said district, hath deposited in this office, the title of a book, the right whereof he claims as proprietor, in the words following, to wit:

"The Second Part; or, A Key to the Higher Degrees of Freemasonry: Giving a clear and correct view of the way and manner of conferring the Degrees of Mark-Master, Past-Master, Most Excellent Master, and Royal Arch Mason, on a Candidate; as practiced in all well-governed Lodges and Chapters, throughout the Globe; together with the means to be used by such as are not Masons, to gain Admission therein:—the whole intended as a guide to the Craft, and a light to the unenlightened. BY A MEMBER OF THE CRAFT. 'Put off thy shoes from off thy feet for the place whereon thou standest is holy ground.'" EXODUS iii.

In conformity to the Act of Congress of the United States, entitled "An Act for the encouragement of learning, by securing the copies of maps, charts, and books, to the authors and proprietors of such copies, during the time therein mentioned:" and also, of the act, entitled "An Act supplementary to an act entitled an act for the encouragement of learning, by securing the copies of maps, charts, and books to the authors and proprietors of such copies, during the time therein mentioned, and extending the benefits thereof to the arts of designing, engraving, and etching historical and other prints."

                                                      W. KEY BOND,
Clerk of the District of Ohio

PREFACE.

THE unfortunate and lamented MORGAN, having published and laid open to the world, his 'ILLUSTRATIONS' of the first part, or three first Degrees of Masonry, the writer of this work conceived the necessity of producing the remaining and Higher Mysteries of the Craft, in order to prevent this Glorious Institution from falling into disrepute among its enemies. The idea held forth by my predecessor, in this rather unpleasant business, I must acknowledge, is illy calculated to wrest the Order from that stigma and reproach, which its enemies are ever ready to heap upon it, which is my present intention; and I here avow that my *only* object in offering this work to the public, is to remove the prejudicial impressions very liable to exist in the minds of the uninitiated, from a perusal of Morgan's work. By presenting the brighter side of the picture, if I effect nothing more, my conscience will be relieved of a duty I conceive I owe the Institution of which I have been, and yet remain, a Member.*

From the painful events attendant on the publication of Morgan, the public will not censure me for withholding my name and place of residence; from these they can also judge of the danger to which *I* should be exposed, in case the Higher Order of Masons should discover me: consequently I shall be pardoned and justified by every candid man, for using every precaution to counteract such an event. If Morgan has been barbarously murdered for revealing the three *lower* Degrees, what fate would be awarded to one who should withdraw the vail, and lay open the four *HIGHER!!* In truth, I tremble while I write; but having formed my design, and I trust from no sinister motive, nothing but the King of Terrors shall prevent me from portraying it on the TRESTLE-BOARD of public opinion; leaving for the public to determine whether the Institution deserves the bitter reproach and contumely it has received, since the 'Affairs at Batavia,' and the 'Abduction of Morgan.'

I have not dared to hint my intentions to a living soul, well knowing that

---

* Although I have been a *Member* of the Craft for many years, the reader will discover, from certain *explanations* annexed to this work, that in all probability I am the only individual on the Globe who could possibly reveal these higher mysteries of the Order, without committing the vilest perjury, by violating *oaths the most sacred.*

no one of the Order could be persuaded to look upon the matter in the light I do, and join me in an undertaking so hazardous; and to repose confidence in any one *not* of the Craft, would be yet more dangerous. It is not my intention to enter into any discussion whatever, upon the merits or demerits of the Institution which has withstood 'the wreck of matter, and the crush of worlds,' but merely to relate my history in a plain, matter-of-fact style; leaving for the public, having the whole matter before them, to be their own judges.

In the following pages, I have deemed it unimportant to annex the LECTURES of the several Degrees (although very instructive), as every one can readily become familiar with them, by visiting Lodges and Chapters, after the knowledge he shall gain from this work. I would here advise the unenlightened reader to perfectly familiarize himself with *one* Degree, before entering upon another; else he might make some blunder on entering a Lodge, by substituting the matter of one Degree for that of another, which would at once prove him an impostor, and might lead to disagreeable consequences.

With a consciousness that the whole artillery of ROYAL ARCH MASONRY will be leveled against me, and held in requisition to find me out, I now proceed to my task, with first informing the world at large, and ROYAL ARCH MASONS in particular, that if any individual who has resided two months in this city should be accused of the authorship of this work, great injustice would be done to such individual; and further, the person who now addresses you, the only person in the whole world who writes this work, or who knows of its being written, was never in his whole life, until within six weeks past, nearer to this City than Batavia, in New York State.

May the Lord grant Peace and Brotherly Love throughout the world. *So mote it be!!*   THE AUTHOR.

CINCINNATI (OHIO), JULY, 1827.

A KEY

TO

THE HIGHER DEGREES

OF

FREEMASONRY.

THE MANNER OF OPENING A LODGE OF MARK-MASTER MASONS.

A MASTER-MASON progressing from the third degree to the fourth, enters an entire new field of operations. The Mark Degree to the Master-Mason, is what the Entered Apprentice's is to the uninitiated. From a regular routine of operations and proceedings, with only some slight difference in grips, words, signs, &c., he enters a field almost totally dissimilar, in every respect. But to our subject.

The Brethren being assembled, and the officers having repaired to their several stations, the Master addresses the Junior Overseer as follows:

Master. Brother Jabal,* are all things in preparation for the work?

Junior Overseer. All things are in readiness, Worshipful.

Master. Then let every Brother present mark well the entering in of the house: *observe your Master!*

The Master now descends from his station, and approaches a small Temple, which has been previously erected on the middle of the floor, with blocks of wood in the shape of bricks, but not half so large. Every mark Lodge is provided with these blocks, and everything fits with such an exact nicety, that the whole can be put together in the space of fifteen minutes, so as to form a perfect miniature of King Solomon's Temple, with all its porticoes and other ornaments. The master approaches the front of this little Temple, which faces the east, and opens a small golden door, when a transparent view is had within, of the *Sanctum Sanctorum* or *Holy of Holies*. Immediately above (yet within the Temple), are two golden Cherubims,† supporting

---

* Jabal was the name of a certain Junior Overseer at the building of King Solomon's Temple, whom this officer, in every Mark-Lodge, represents.—See Note, page 88.

† Over the ark (which contained the manna), was the mercy-seat and it was the covering of it. It was all made of solid gold, and of the thickness of an hand's breadth. At the two ends of it were two cherubims, looking inward toward each other, with wings expanded, which, embracing the whole circumference of the mercy-seat, did meet on each side in the middle: all of which was made of the same mass, without joining any of the

F

between them a KEY STONE, with a circle of eight letters on it, which will be explained hereafter. The Master then kneels, and while viewing this interior illumination, repeats the following:

"Great Architect of the universe, we approach thy Holy Tabernacle with a sincere desire that our works may tend to magnify Thy Holy Name, and to disseminate the cement of Brotherly Love, throughout the secret recesses of the human heart. Grant that our work may be approved in thy sight, and finally that each of us may be fitted and prepared for 'that spiritual building, that house not made with hands, eternal in the Heavens!'"

Response by the Brethren. *"So mote it be!"*

The preceding prayer is not universally used on this occasion;—the following is often substituted:

"Wherefore, Brethren, lay aside all malice, and guile, and hypocrisies, and envies, and all evil speakings. If so be, ye have tasted that the Lord is gracious, to whom coming as unto a living stone, disallowed indeed of men but chosen of God, and precious; ye also, as living stones, be ye built up a spiritual house, an holy priesthood, to offer up sacrifices acceptable to God. Wherefore, also, it is contained in the Scriptures, Behold, I lay in Zion, for a foundation, a tried stone, a precious corner stone, a sure foundation; he that believeth shall not make haste to pass it over. Unto you, therefore, which believe, it is an honor; and even to them which be disobedient, the stone which the builders disallowed, the same is made the head of the corner. Brethren, this is the will of God, that with well doing you put to silence the ignorance of foolish men. As free, and not using your liberty for a cloak of maliciousness, but as the servants of God. Honor all men, love the brotherhood, fear God."

During the rehearsal of one of the preceding prayers, the Brethren all kneel around the Temple, and at the conclusion, they all arise, and each in his turn kneels in front of the golden door, as they pass around; and while viewing the golden cherubims and other beauties within, he exclaims, "H. T. W. S. S. T. K. S."

Having gone through with these ceremonies, the Brethren all standing in a circle around the Temple, the Master proceeds to his station, and holds up to the view of the Brethren, a KEY STONE, with the above initials on it, which he reads aloud thus: 'He That Was Slain, Soars To Kindred Spirits;'—and repeats, 'He That Was Slain Soars To Kindred Spirits.' This has allusion to the ancient Grand Master, Hiram, whose fatal catastrophe is explained in the Third Degree. The origin of this Key Stone, with these

---

parts by solder. Here it was, where t' e *Shechinah*, or divine presence, rested both in the tabernacle and temple, and was visibly seen in the appearance of a cloud over it. And hence it is, that God is so often said in Scripture to dwell between the Cherubims; that is, between the Cherubims on the mercy-seat, because there was the seat or throne of the visible appearance of his glory among them.—H. PRIDEAUX, vol. 1, p. 298.

initials on it, is very curious, and will be explained in its proper place. The Master now proclaims the Lodge open as follows:

Master. Brethren, we are again assembled around this Altar of Peace. May the extended wings of the golden Cherubims continually remind us of the unbounded latitude of Masonic Charity. May the Lord prosper our work, to the honor of His Holy Name.

Response by the Brethren. ' *So mote it be!*'

Master. ' Observe your Master.'

The Brethren all join in giving the *due-guard, sign, and clap.*

Master. I now proclaim this Lodge duly and truly prepared for labor. The Junior Overseer will give notice hereof to the Tyler, and the Brethren will retire to their several stations.

The golden door is now closed, the Brethren take their stations, and thus ends the ceremony of opening a Lodge of Mark-Master Masons.

FOURTH DEGREE OF MASONRY.

THE MODE AND MANNER OF CONFERRING THE DEGREE OF MARK-MASTER MASON ON A CANDIDATE—IT BEING THE FOURTH DEGREE OF MASONRY; TOGETHER WITH THE MEANS TO BE USED BY SUCH AS ARE NOT MASONS, TO GAIN ADMISSION INTO ANY LODGE OF MARK-MASTERS ON THE FACE OF THE GLOBE.

A MASTER-MASON who has petitioned the Chapter to have conferred on him the Degree of a Mark-Master, is ballotted for, as in the preceding Degrees; and if accepted, will be conducted into a private room, and asked the following questions, by the Master Overseer:

Master Overseer. Brother A. B., having progressed in safety to the third and last round of *Jacob's ladder,* do you wish to proceed further?

Candidate. I do, with your permission.

Master Overseer. Do you solemnly promise, upon your honor as a Master-Mason, to conform to the rules and customs observed by the Ancient Patriarchs who have traveled this road before you?

Candidate. I do most cheerfully, with your permission.

The Overseer then informs the Candidate that he is about entering a new apartment of the Temple, and recommends him to betray no fears during the numerous trials and difficulties he is about to encounter; that all who have traveled this way before him, have bravely submitted to the same, &c. If the Candidate makes no objection, he is deprived of all his clothing, except his shirt and drawers (the latter are furnished when the Candidate is without them), and his hands are tied closely behind him, by placing their backs together, and winding a strong cord *four times* around his arms about midway between the elbow and wrist.* (It is necessary to pay strict attention to this ceremony, as it is the basis of a *Mark-Master's Sign:* remember his hands are placed *behind* him, *back to back*.) The Candidate is then enshrouded in a Purple Robe, after which he is closely blindfolded, by a bandage wrapped *four times* over his eyes, in which situation he is conducted into the Lodge by the Overseer.

The Master now informs the Candidate that an *Oath* must be taken, before he can progress farther, whereupon he is caused to mount a platform erected for the purpose, by a flight of *four steps*. There is also an altar placed on this platform, on which lies the Holy Bible, opened at the fourth chapter of St. Mark. The candidate is caused to kneel on both knees, with his face (i. e. one cheek,†) resting on the Holy Bible, when the following oath is administered by the Master:

"In the name of God, and the Holy Prophets, I solemnly swear and affirm, that I will keep inviolate the mysteries pertaining to the Degree of a Mark-Master Mason, within my own breast, except when only in company with Mark-Masters. That in my intercourse with the world, I will use my utmost endeavors to prevent my Brother Mark-Masters from deviating from that line of rectitude taught them in this Holy Sanctuary. Lastly, that I will never give the Mark-Master's GRAND HAILING-SIGN OF DISTRESS, except in *actual distress*.‡ In the name of God, and the Holy Prophets."

This constitutes the Oath of a Mark-Master Mason. The cord is now taken from the arms of the Candidate, but his hands are held in the same situation behind him, *back to back*, by some of the Brethren, while the Master instructs him in the *Due-Guard Sign* of a Mark-Master, which is by bringing his hands around before him, and letting them meet (crossing each other so as to make a loud clap, *four times* in succession. Now is the proper time for the reader to perfect himself in this *Due-Guard Sign:* place your hands behind you *with their backs together; then bring them round together crossing, making the palms hollow, so as to make a loud clap by the concussion;* and this repeat *four times:* this is called the *Mark-Master's Due-Guard and Clap*, and will always be exacted before any one not known as a Mark-Master can enter a Mark-Lodge, as the GRAND HAILING-SIGN cannot be given except in "actual distress," as specified in the Oath.)

The Candidate is now informed that this *Due-Guard Sign* has reference to the situation of his hands when he took upon himself the Oath; and the

---

* Of binding and loosing—*Bind not two sins together*, Ec. vii, 8.

† *Jabal* or *Iobel* (Hebrew),—falling away—or bringing—or building—or a *cheek*. Lamech's son by Adah: father of such as dwell in tents, and such as have cattle. See GEN. iv. 20.

‡ This sign is not even allowed to be given in the Lodge, notwithstanding it is almost impossible that any one should notice it, as the reader will discover.

clapping them together four times, has strict allusion to the fourth Degree of Masonry. This Due-Guard Sign is allowed in mixed companies, as no one could suspect any meaning to it, except a Mark-Master Mason. The author of this work recollects of seeing this often given before he ever sat in a Mark-Lodge, and very likely the reader does the same. It should be done in a careless manner, in order that the unenlightened may not notice it. A Mark-Mason may know another by merely clapping with the hands four times, the same as applauding an actor on the Stage in a theater, without placing his hands first behind him at all; but this will not answer for one who would go in a Mark-Lodge, as there they scrutinize very closely, and if one be deficient in recollecting the way in which his hands were tied behind him, *back to back*, when he took the Oath, this deficiency would be certain evidence that he was an impostor, and unworthy the privilege he claimed.

The Candidate is then told that his present situation represents the time previous to the creation of the world, and the Master takes him by the hand, and says:

Master. Brother A. B., I now present you with the right-hand of a Brother, and also with the grip of this degree.

Here the Master takes the Candidate by the right-hand, and presses the nail of his right thumb into the last joint of the third finger of the Candidate (i. e. the joint farthest from the nail), and requests the Candidate to do the same—which done, the Master says:

Master. This, Brother, is the Grip of a Mark-Master Mason, and its name is emblematical of your present state. It is CHAOS; and as yet, Brother CHAOS, you are in the Dark. Should you, in your travels, hear the word CHAOS pronounced, whether in darkness or daylight, you may rest assured a brother Mark-Master utters it, and is in deep distress; and this word you are entitled to use when in like situation, *and then only*, accompanied by the GRAND HAILING-SIGN OF DISTRESS, which you will hereafter be instructed in.*

The Candidate is now divested of his bandages, and conducted down the four steps directly in front of the Temple, when the Master presents him with a Chisel and Mallet, which are the working tools of this Degree; and placing the edge of the Chisel on the right temple of the Candidate, orders him to "*strike and receive the mark!*" The Candidate of course declines, and this part of the ceremony is thus explained to him by the Master at the time:

Master. Brother, it was not my intention that you should strike the blow; but this is intended to teach you through life, to withhold your arm, when raised to injure a fellow-being, especially a Brother, the same as if raised against yourself. We are all of the same family, and are all the children of the

---

* It is certainly a singular coincidence, that this word of distress, and its accompanying Grand Hailing-Sign, should have so nearly the same sound; as the reader will discover they have when he learns the Sign—Chaos—K. S.

same Great Parent; and all should strive to "do unto others, as we would that others should do unto us."

The Candidate is then caused to kneel on both knees, when the golden door is opened, which presents to his view the illuminations within the Temple, when the Master addresses him as follows:

Master. Brother A. B., you now discover the LIGHT by which Mark-Master Masons work. You are now about to be invested with SECRETS, intrusted only in the faithful breasts of Mark-Masters throughout the Globe; and which will entitle you to, and insure their respect and esteem, wheresoever dispersed around the known world. The illuminated Temple before you, is a perfect miniature of King Solomon's at Jerusalem, the Holy City; the KEY STONE, supported by the Cherubims with expanded wings, is the main support in all arches, built by operative Masons: with us, as Mark-Masters, it it is emblematical of the BINDING LINK OF BROTHERLY LOVE, which unites,† in one strong CHAIN, all who have attained to this Honorary Degree. This STONE, my Brother, is also typical of the Stone which was rejected by the builders of old, and in modern days, which stone is TRUTH. Truth is the Stone which unworthy builders reject, and which is to become the "head of the Corner." "He that hath an ear to hear let him hear." "To him that overcometh will I give to eat of the HIDDEN MANNA, and will give him a WHITE STONE, and in the Stone a *new name written,* which no man knoweth save him that receiveth it." "The Stone which the builders refused, is become the head Stone of the corner." "Did ye never read in the Scriptures, The Stone which the builders rejected, is become the head of the corner?" "And have ye not read this Scripture, The Stone which the builders rejected, is become the head of the corner?" "What is this, then, that is written, The Stone which the builders rejected, is become the head of the corner?" (The GOD OF TRUTH, my Brother.) "This is the Stone which was set at naught of you, builders, which has become the head of the corner."

"Then he brought me back the way of the gate of the outward Sanctuary, which looketh toward the EAST; and it was shut." [Here the Master shuts the golden gate, or door.] "Then said the Lord unto me, This gate shall be shut, it shall not be opened, and no man shall enter in by it; because the Lord, the God of Israel, hath entered in by it, therefore it shall be shut. It is for the Prince, the Prince he shall sit in it to eat bread before the Lord; he shall enter by the way of the porch of that gate, and shall go out by the way of the same. And the Lord said unto me, Son of Man, mark well, and behold with thine eyes, and hear with thine ears, all that I say unto thee concerning all the ordinances of the house of the Lord, and all the laws thereof; and mark well the entering in of the house, with every going forth of the Sanctuary.'

The Master now reopens the golden gate, and addresses the Candidate as follows:

---

* Or should unite, is frequently added by the Master, and very properly too.

Master. Brother A. B., I now have the pleasure to present you with the "*New Name,*" which "no man knoweth, saving him that receiveth it;" and which is contained in the "*white stone*" which "the builders rejected." The initials you discover, are H. T. W. S. S. T. K. S.—These, as Mark-Master Masons, we read thus: He That Was Slain, Soars To Kindred Spirits—He That Was Slain, Soars To Kindred Spirits.

'These initials were placed on the Key Stone of the *Ninth Arch,* by King Solomon, to commemorate the melancholy death of Hiram, an account of which you have received in the preceding Degree. This Key Stone had its origin as follows: A skillful workman, at the building of King Solomon's Temple, named Kerim, after the death of his Grand Master, Hiram, held a consultation with King Solomon, on the subject of the most appropriate manner in which the worth and excellence of this truly great and good man, might be handed down to posterity. After considerable discussion, it was agreed that these initials should be engraved on the Key Stone of the Ninth Arch; and their signification communicated to those only of this Degree, forever; you are therefore cautioned, my Brother, to divulge this mystery to no one, either within or without the Lodge, except in the following manner: Should you wish to know if a stranger be a Mark-Master, you will say audibly, "*He.*" No matter if the room be full of strangers, at the time, no one except a Mark-Master will notice you. If there be one present, he will say, "*That.*" You will then approach him, if there be others present, and in a low tone say, "*Was.*" He will then (if he be a Mark-Master,) say, "*Slain;*" —when you will reply, "*Soars;*" and he, "*To;*"—you, "*Kindred;*" —he, "*Spirits.*" This much will satisfy each of you that the other is a Mark-Master Mason; but it is necessary to speak in a voice that cannot be overheard by the bystanders. This, Brother, is the only way in which you are ever to give the signification of these initials, except you preside as Master over a Lodge, in which case you are allowed to repeat them twice at the opening of a Lodge, and twice to a Candidate, as I have done to you this evening.'

At this stage of the proceedings, the Candidate is presented with a chair, and requested by the Master to take his seat, which he is very willing to do, after kneeling for so long a time. The Master then proceeds:

Master. Having progressed thus far, we now proceed to the *Sanctum Sanctorum* or *Holy of Holies.* You here discover the extended wings of the two Cherubims, which guard and protect the heavenly *Manna,* sent down from God out of Heaven. This *Manna,* Brother, has been handed down by Mark-Master Masons, since the Children of Israel sojourned in the wilderness; and without a portion of this, no Mark-Lodge could be established.*

Here the Master reaches his arm through the golden gate, opens the tab-

---

* A Jar of the ancient Manna, was actually preserved, and used in Mark-Lodges, as far down as 413 years after the Christian era; but no one in his sober senses, will doubt that the Manna used in *modern* Mark-Lodges, is of modern production.

ernacle, and takes therefrom a pot of manna, and presenting a morsel of it to the Candidate, in a silver spoon, proceeds as follows:

Master. "To him that overcometh will I give to eat of the *hidden Manna,*" saith the Lord: take, eat, and praise His Holy Name.

Response by the Brethren. *"And praise His Holy Name!"*

The pot of Manna and the silver spoon are then replaced in the Tabernacle, and the golden door is closed; when the Master addresses the Candidate as follows:

Master. You will now arise, my Brother, and receive the Mark-Master's GRAND HAILING-SIGN OF DISTRESS.

It will be discovered, that the Master cannot give the Sign, without forfeiting his Oath, not being in *"actual distress;"* he consequently teaches the Candidate as follows:

Master. This sign is made, Brother, by raising your right arm in a position horizontal with the earth, and moving your right fore-finger (the rest being closed) so as to form the letter K in the air, and then a period, or a dot after it, and then let your arm drop down by your side; you will then raise it, as before, and with your finger form the letter S in the air, with a period or dot after it, and then drop your arm as before; and this is the *Grand Hailing-Sign of Distress* of a Mark-Master Mason. Now, Brother, please give this Sign, that the Brethren present may see that you understand it.

Of nineteen cases in twenty, the Candidate raises his arm to do as required, when a Brother seizes it, and the Master says as follows:

Master. Let this be a striking lesson to you, Brother. You have sworn never to give this Sign, except in "actual distress," and I have done the same; which accounts for my giving it to you verbally; you was about to perjure yourself, when a Brother stayed your arm and prevented you. Let this teach you to step forth, and stay the arm of a Brother, when about to commit any rash act; and to use your utmost endeavors to keep him from falling into evil. Remember your Oath, Brother!—(A Candidate generally feels the full force of these remarks.]

It is unnecessary to inform the reader of common discernment, that these letters, K. S., are the initials of the *Key Stone.*—The Candidate is now placed on the opposite side of the Temple, with his face fronting the Master, who thus addresses him:

Master. Brother A. B., you have now arrived at a station attained but by few of your Brethren,* and it is your embounden duty to guard against all immoralities in your life and conduct, which might prejudice the world against our excellent Institution, or serve as an apology to your Brethren of a lower Degree, for following your example. You will alleviate the suf-

---

* This charge has been handed down from very remote times, when, no doubt, it was *true.* Very *many* are admitted to this Degree in modern days—very many more than profit by the excellent lessons they receive.

ferings of the distressed, by contributing to their relief, if within your power, and if not, by sympathizing with their distresses. I now have the pleasure to present you with the *working tools* of your profession. The working tools of a Mark-Master Mason, are the Chisel and Mallet, which are thus moralized:

The *Chisel* morally demonstrates the advantages of discipline and education. The mind, in its original state, like the diamond, is rude and unpolished; but as the effect of the Chisel on the external coat soon presents to view the latent beauties of the diamond, so education discovers the latent virtues of the mind, and draws them forth to range the large field of matter and space,—to display the summit of human knowledge—our duty to God and to man.

The *Mallet* morally teaches to correct irregularities, and to reduce man to a proper level; so that by quiet deportment, he may, in the school of discipline, learn to be content. What the Mallet is to the workman, enlightened reason is to the passions: it curbs ambition, depresses envy, it moderates anger, and it encourages good dispositions; whence arises, among good Masons, that comely order,

"Which nothing earthly gives, or can destroy—
The soul's calm sunshine, and the heart-felt joy."

The Master now resumes his station in the East, and says:

Master. Brother Master Overseer, you will take charge of the Candidate, and return with him to the Lodge in due season.

The Candidate is then reconducted to the private room; his Robe is taken off, and he puts on his own clothes—when he is again taken into the Lodge, and the Master, through the hands of the Master Overseer, presents him with a lamb-skin, or white leather apron, and the Overseer teaches him how to wear it, which is simply by tying it on, and so placing the strings by its several corners as imperfectly to form the letters K. S., crossing each other. The Candidate is again placed on the platform, with his face toward the Master, who gives him the following

CHARGE.

'BROTHER: I congratulate you on having been thought worthy of being promoted to this honorable degree of Masonry. Permit me to impress it on your mind, that your assiduity should ever be commensurate with your duties, which become more and more extensive as you advance in Masonry.

'The situation to which you are now promoted will draw upon you not only the scrutinizing eyes of the world at large, but those also of your Brethren, on whom this Degree of Masonry has not been conferred: all will be justified in expecting your conduct and behavior to be such as may with safety be imitated.

'In the honorable character of Mark-Master Mason, it is more particularly your duty to endeavor to let your conduct in the world, as well as in the Lodge, and among your brethren, be such as may stand the test of the Grand Overseer's Square; that you may not, like the unfinished and imperfect work of the negligent and unfaithful of former times, be rejected and thrown aside, as unfit for 'that spiritual building, that house not made with hands, eternal in the Heavens.'

'While such is your conduct, should misfortune assail you, should friends forsake you, should envy traduce your good name, and malice persecute you; yet may you have confidence, that among Mark-Master Masons, you will find friends who will administer relief to your distresses, and comfort your afflictions; ever bearing in mind, as a consolation under all the frowns of fortune, and as an encouragement to hope better prospects, that *the stone which the builders rejected* (possessing merits to them unknown) *became the chief stone of the corner.*'

This concludes the Charge, and the Candidate is conducted down from the platform, and takes his seat; and this is the concluding ceremony at the conferring of this Degree. If there is no further business before the Lodge, it is closed in the following manner:

Master. Brother Jabal, are all things in preparation for the conclusion of our work?

Junior Overseer. All things are in preparation, Worshipful.

Master. Then let every Brother present mark well the entering in of the gate, with every going forth of the sanctuary. Observe your Master!

The Master here descends from his station, and proceeds to the Temple, as in opening; and having opened the golden door, while the Brethren all kneel around in a circle, he recites the lengthy parable beginning with, 'For the Kingdom of Heaven is like unto a man that is an householder, which went out early in the morning,' &c., which it is needless here to insert, as it can be found in Webb's 'MASONIC MONITOR,' page 91. The Master then holds up the Key Stone and says, ' He;'—his next Brother says, 'Was;'— the next, 'Slain';—and so on until the last word is said of which the letters on the Key Stone are the initials; and if there be more than eight Brethren present, the one next to the seventh Brother from the Master begins over again, and this method is continued, if there are fifty in the room, until each Brother has pronounced a word. This is in accordance with the idea held forth in the parable just referred to, concerning those who came in ' at the eleventh hour,' receiving as much wages as those who 'have borne the burden and heat of the day.' See Monitor, pages 91 and 92.

The Brethren now all arise, and march around the Temple, until they have finished singing the Mark-Master's Song, which may also be found

MASCNRY ILLUSTRATED. 95

in the Monitor, pages 93 and 94. Having concluded the song, the Master says:

Master. Brethren, we are about to separate from this Altar of Peace. May the extended wings of the Cherubims continually remind us of the unbounded latitude of Masonic Charity. May the Lord prosper our work, to the honor of his Holy Name.

Response by the Brethren : ' *So mote it be !*'

Master. I now proclaim this Lodge duly and truly closed. May we all, my Brothers, conduct ourselves as men and Masons, until we again assemble around this Altar of Peace

Response : ' *So mote it be!*'

Here the ceremony closes, and the Brethren disperse, except the Tyler, whose duty it is to take due care of the materials in and about the Temple, and to take the Temple itself to pieces, and place them in a box under lock and key, lest Master-Masons meeting in the same room on other nights, might see them, and make some improper discoveries.

I might swell out the pages, by giving the LECTURES of the several Degrees, but as they are merely explanatory of the ceremonies here related, and of certain circumstances connected with the building of King Solomon's Temple, I shall only make this work what it purports to be, a 'KEY,' &c. wherewith may be unlocked the door of the Masonic Temple, through which any one may enter who will follow the rules here laid down.

THE MEANS TO BE USED BY SUCH AS ARE NOT MASONS, TO GAIN ADMISSION INTO ANY LODGE OF MARK-MASTERS ON THE FACE OF THE GLOBE.

Nothing is more apt to make one's heart feel timorous, than to attempt to pass on his fellow-being a falsehood for a truth—or a base counterfeit coin for a genuine one; more especially when connected with the subject of this work, which has performed its midnight rites in secret conclave for centuries past, defying, as it were, the searching and scrutinizing eyes of the whole world! This timorousness must be overcome before any one attempts to go into a Mark-Lodge. He must take unto himself a resolution which cannot be shaken off at the door, otherwise he will quake and tremble, and have only his labor for his pains: but if he will follow exactly the rules here laid down, with boldness and resolution, no Mark-Lodge on the Globe DARE refuse him admission.

On proceeding to the door of a Mark-Lodge, the Tyler will be found outside, with a naked sword, as in the Lower Degrees. After bidding the

Tyler good evening, you can ask him on what Degree the Lodge is open. If the Mark-Master's, you can tell him you are a stranger,* and would like to be examined. If you see an apron lying near, put it on with as much freedom as possible, and betray no fears or uneasiness—as this would excite suspicion. The Tyler will then give four knocks at the door, which will be answered by four from within, when it will open, and the Tyler will whisper in the ear of the Junior Overseer that 'a Brother wishes to be examined.' The door will again close, and presently the three Overseers (sometimes but two) will come to you from another door, and conduct you into the private room where Candidates are first taken—when the following will be your course to pursue: Address yourself to either of the Overseers, and say, 'I am a Mark-Master, and a stranger; therefore I wish to be examined.' When the Overseer to whom you address yourself, will ask, 'Where was you made a Mark-Master?'

Applicant. In front of the Temple.
Overseer. What was between you and the Temple, at the time?
Applicant. The golden door.
Overseer. Give me the grand hailing-sign of a Mark-Master.
Applicant. That is beyond my power, at this time, Brother.
Overseer. Have you any other sign to dispose of?
Applicant. I have, with your assistance, Brother.
Overseer. How will you dispose of it?
Applicant. By dividing the circle.
Overseer. Proceed.

[Here give the *due-guard sign and clap once*, when the Overseer will do the same; you will repeat, when he will also repeat, which will complete the four times.]

Overseer. What do you call this sign, Brother?
Applicant. The due-guard sign and clap of a Mark-Master.
Overseer. What further have you to convince me you are a Mark-Master?
Applicant. A grip, Brother.
Overseer. Give me it.
Applicant.—[Taking him by the right-hand, and pressing your thumb-nail into the upper joint of his third finger, i. e. the joint farthest from the nail]: This is the grip of a Mark-Master.
Overseer. By what *name* is this grip designated, Brother?
Applicant. By a name similar in sound to the *letters* made in the air by a Mark-Master in distress, accompanied by the grand hailing-sign.

---

* If you are known by many, or any of the members, it would be better not to apply for admission except just after you return from a journey; and then sometime previous to the meeting of the Lodge, tell them you have taken the degree during your absence.

Overseer. Give me it, Brother.
Applicant. I will, by dividing the *square.*
Overseer. Proceed, Brother.
Applicant. OS.—*Overseer.* CHA.—*Applicant.* CHA.—*Overseer.* OS.—*applicant.* CHAOS.—*Overseer.* Right, Brother Chaos, I greet you in the name of the Holy St. Mark, and all Mark-Masters throughout the Globe.*

You will then be reported to the Lodge by the Overseers, as a regular Mark-Master Mason, and introduced accordingly. On entering, you will proceed to the center of the floor, and give the due-gard, sign and clap in full, that the brethren may be also satisfied you are entitled to the privilege you have gained, and then take a seat. The examination by the Overseers seldom extends beyond what is here laid down—though in some instances it proceeds to the *new name* on the Key Stone, which by this time the reader can repeat as well as the brightest Mark-Master; but he must always take especial care, should the Overseer touch on this subject, to utter but *one* of the words at a time, and insist on the next one being spoken by the Overseer, should he refuse, which is sometimes done, the more fully to test the qualifications of a visiting Brother. By adhering strictly to the rules here laid down, the reader, if sex or age does not oppose, can visit any Mark Lodge on the Globe, of whatever country or nation. On learning the *Lecture* of this Degree, it will be found very interesting and instructive. It is divided into two sections. The *first section* explains the manner of convocating and opening a Mark-Master's Lodge. It teaches the stations and duties of the respective officers, and recapitulates the mystic ceremony of introducing a Candidate. In the *second section*, the Mark-Master is particularly instructed in the origin and history of this Degree, and the indispensable obligation he is under to stretch forth his assisting hand to the relief of an indigent and worthy Brother, to a certain and specified extent. The progress made in architecture, particularly in the reign of Solomon, is remarked; the number of artists employed in building the Temple of Jerusalem, and the privileges they enjoyed, are specified; the mode of rewarding merit, and of punishing the guilty, are pointed out; and the marks of distinction, which were conferred on our ancient Brethren, as the rewards of excellence, are particularly named.—*End of Fourth Degree.*

---

* This is properly the last grip in Masonry; but since the publication of 'Jachin and Boaz,' some Past-Masters press their thumb between this third finger and the little finger, and call it the *pass*-grip of a Past-Master, without a name, however; and then passing the thumb along to the third or last joint from the end of the little finger, press in the nail and call it *Chibbilum.* This is only practiced among a few modern Masons, and does not belong to ancient Masonry.

FIFTH DEGREE OF MASONRY.

THE MODE AND MANNER OF CONFERRING THE DEGREE OF PAST-MASTER MASON ON A CANDIDATE—IT BEING THE FIFTH DEGREE OF MASONRY; TOGETHER WITH THE MEANS TO BE USED BY SUCH AS ARE NOT MASONS, TO GAIN ADMISSION INTO ANY LODGE OF PAST-MASTERS ON THE FACE OF THE GLOBE.

This Degree will be found very uninteresting to the general reader, as it merely relates to the regulation of Lodges, the mode of laying corner stones, installing officers, constituting new Lodges, ceremonies observed at funerals, consecrations, &c. &c.; the principal part of which may be found in Webb's Monitor, from page 94 to 145.

As it would be folly to present to the public what is already before them, I shall merely give the manner in which this Degree is conferred, which will enable any one to visit a Lodge of Past-Masters, and seek such further elucidation of the subject as his curiosity may prompt. This Degree is conferred on every Master of a Lodge previous to his installation.

A Candidate about to take this Degree, is conducted into the Lodge without ceremony, and caused to kneel before the tabernacle, with his hands resting on the Holy Bible, in the following manner: he lays his left-hand on the left page, and his right-hand on the right page, letting the end of the fore-finger of each hand touch each other, with the thumbs pointing in a straight line across the page, toward each other (i. e. the way the lines run in the book), and their ends also touching each other; which forms a perfect TRIANGLE (with the exception of a slight curve in the middle of the base where the thumbs meet) as any one may readily discover, by placing his hands in that situation. In order to form as perfect a triangle as possible, the fingers adjoining the foremost ones, i. e. the second fingers, and the two longest on the hands, are kept close to the fore ones, from the roots to the ends, and the ends of these longest (which reach somewhat further than the fore ones), must be suffered to barely graze each other, taking care also to press the ends of the thumbs together until the end of each nail meets. In this situation, the Master administers the following

OATH.

"In the name of God, and the Holy Prophets, I solemnly swear, that I will recognize no Brother, as Past-Master, except he first prove himself such by the TRIANGLE OF TRUTH; and that I will keep inviolate the sign and words of a Past-Master, except when in the presence of those only who are legally in possession of the same, and then only, except by the Triangle of Truth. In the name of God, and the Holy Prophets!"

This oath being taken, the Candidate is told to arise, when the Master addresses him thus:

"Brother—Previous to your investiture, it is necessary that you should signify your assent to those ancient charges and regulations which point out the duty of a Master of a Lodge."

The Master then reads a summary of the ancient charges, to the Candidate, as follows:

"I. You agree to be a good man and true, and strictly to obey the moral law.

"II. You agree to be a peaceable subject, and cheerfully to conform to the laws of the country in which you reside.

"III. You promise not to be concerned in plots and conspiracies against government, but patiently to submit to the decisions of the supreme legislature.

"IV. You agree to pay a proper respect to the civil magistrate, to work diligently, live creditably, and act honorably by all men.

"V. You agree to hold in veneration the original rulers and patrons of the order of Masonry, and their regular successors, supreme and subordinate according to their stations; and to submit to the awards and resolutions of your brethren when convened, in every case consistent with the constitutions of the order.

"VI. You agree to avoid private piques and quarrels, and to guard against intemperance and excess.

"VII. You agree to be cautious in carriage and behavior, courteous to your Brethren, and faithful to your Lodge.

"VIII. You promise to respect genuine Brethren, and to discountenance impostors, and all dissenters from the original plan of Masonry.

"IX. You agree to promote the general good of society, to cultivate the social virtues, and to propagate the knowledge of the art.

"X. You promise to pay homage to the Grand Master for the time being, and to his officers, when duly installed; and strictly to conform to every edict of the Grand Lodge, or general assembly of Masons, that is not subversive of the principles and ground-work of Masonry.

"XI. You admit that it is not in the power of any man, or body of men, to make innovations in the body of Masonry.

"XII. You promise a regular attendance on the committees and communications of the Grand Lodge, on receiving proper notice; and to pay attention to all the duties of masonry, on convenient occasions.

"XIII. You admit that no new Lodge shall be formed without permission of the Grand Lodge; and that no countenance be given to any irregular Lodge, or to any person clandestinely initiated therein, being contrary to the ancient charges of the order.

"XIV. You admit that no person can be regularly made a Mason in, or admitted a member of, any regular Lodge, without previous notice, and due inquiry into his character.

"XV. You agree that no visitors shall be received into your Lodge without due examination, and producing proper vouchers of their having been initiated into a regular Lodge."

After giving the foregoing charges, the Master addresses the Candidate as follows:

"Brother A. B.,—Do you submit to these charges, and promise to support these regulations, as Past-Masters have done in all ages before you?"

Having signified his cordial submission, the Master continues:

"Brother—in consequence of your cheerful conformity to the charges and regulations of the order, you are now intrusted with the sign and words of this Degree, which were established by our three ancient Grand Masters at Jerusalem a short time previous to the completion of the Temple, with the fullest confidence that you will keep and preserve the same inviolate."*

The Master here gives the sign, which is done by placing his hands in the position in which they were when the oath was taken, and raising them so as to let the ends of the thumbs, where they meet, rest about on the middle of the nose, and the two ends of the fore-fingers that meet, on the head directly over the forehead; at the same time looking through the triangle thus formed, at the lower angles, at the Candidate; and pronouncing the words, "TRIANGLE OF TRUTH."

The Candidate being taught this, the Master says:

"This, Brother, is the Sign, and these the words, of a Past-Master, which you have sworn never to give or receive, except by the *Triangle of Truth*, which is the manner in which you receive them; nor then, except when only in the Presence of Past-Masters."

The Master now forms the triangle again, and raising his hands as described above (the Candidate being taught the same), looks through at the Candidate, and says:

'Brother—I now behold you within the Triangle of Truth—and may the All-Seeing Eye ever thus find you.'

The Master then takes his station, and delivers a charge almost the same as the one addressed to the Master at his installation, which may be found in the Monitor, pages 121 and 122, and which it is needless here to transcribe. The Candidate is then presented with a *Triangle*, which is his peculiar insignia, and takes his seat. There being no other business, the Lodge is then closed.

This Degree is conferred upon many who have not taken the Mark De-

---

* By a reference to the Monitor, page 114, it will be seen that this language is nearly the same as that used at the installation of a Master of a Lodge.

gree, as all Masters of Lodges (I now mean Master's Lodges), must receive this prior to their installation; but no one can progress farther than this Degree without first taking the Mark: and in fact this Degree seems more properly to belong to the lower Degrees than to the higher ones—and I am inclined to think, that, *anciently*, this was counted the *Fourth* Degree, although I have no Masonic authority for so believing, or a single second to such a belief, that I am aware of. The Lecture of this Degree is dividde into five sections, the leading features of which may be seen in the Monitor from page 96 to 145.

THE MEANS TO BE USED BY SUCH AS ARE NOT MASONS, TO GAIN ADMISSION INTO ANY LODGE OF PAST-MASTERS ON THE FACE OF THE GLOBE.

It is a very easy matter to enter a Lodge of Past-Masters, if you have the sign correctly, as that is generally all that is required. Sometimes the words are resorted to, and lest the reader might not fairly understand the ceremony to be performed, I shall here lay it down so plainly that he cannot fail to understand it.*

You will proceed to the door of the Lodge, which you will find guarded by the Tyler with a drawn sword, as in the Mark Degree, and on requesting to be admitted, he will give *five knocks* at the door, which will be answered by the same number from within; when the door will be opened, and the Tyler will whisper your request to the Brother who opens it, when the door will again be closed. During the interval, you can ask the Tyler on what Degree the Lodge is open, and if he says the Fifth, or Past-Master's, you will proceed as follows, when the person sent out to examine you, has conducted you into the private room, as stated in the last Degree:

Applicant. I am the Past-Master, and wish to enter this Lodge of Past-Masters.

Past-Master. How am I to know you are such?

Applicant. By this. [Here place your hands before you, as when the oath is taken.]

Past-Master. Have you anything more, Brother?

Applicant. I have. [Here raise your hands, as before stated, and looking through the triangle, the Mason will say],

Past-Master. What is that, Brother?

Applicant. The Triangle of Truth. [Here bring your hands down with a flap on each thigh.]

---

* I purpose, in the second edition of this work, to provide *plates*, as I find it a very difficult matter to describe all the niceties accompanying the Signs, in writing. I should have provided them for this edition, but for the fear that the engraving of them might lead to my detection, which would be a destructive event.

The Mason will then be fully satisfied, and introduce you into the Lodge when you will proceed to the middle of the floor and give the sign above-named, that the Brethren may be convinced of your claim; but by all means avoid pronouncing the words at the time. You will barely raise your hands to your eyes, preserving the triangle, and then letting them drop on your thighs with a flap, take a seat.

SIXTH DEGREE OF MASONRY.

THE MODE AND MANNER OF CONFERRING THE DEGREE OF MOST EXCELLENT MASTER-MASON ON A CANDIDATE—IT BEING THE SIXTH DEGREE OF MASONRY; TOGETHER WITH THE MEANS TO BE USED BY SUCH AS ARE NOT MASONS, TO GAIN ADMISSION INTO ANY LODGE OF MOST EXCELLENT MASTERS ON THE FACE OF THE GLOBE.

ANCIENTLY, none but the meritorious and praiseworthy; none but those who through diligence and industry had progressed far toward perfection; none but those who had been seated in the *Oriental Chair*,* by the unanimous suffrages of their Brethren—were admitted to this Degree of Masonry. In its original establishment, when the Temple of Jerusalem was finished, and the fraternity celebrated the cap-stone with great joy, it is demonstrable that none but those who had proved themselves complete masters of their profession were admitted to this honor; and indeed the duties incumbent on every Mason who is accepted and acknowledged as a Most Excellent Master, are such as render it indispensable that he should have a perfect knowledge of all the preceding Degrees.

A Lodge of Most Excellent Masters is opened as follows: The Brethren form themselves into an oblong square around the temple (on which is placed a golden tabernacle, with staves by which it can be carried), as in the Mark Degree, all standing and uncovered: when the Most Excellent Master presiding says: 'The earth is the Lord's and the fullness thereof; the world, and they that dwell therein.'

The Brother next him says: 'For he has founded it upon the seas, and, established it upon the floods.'

The next Brother proceeds: 'Who shall ascend into the hill of the Lord? and who shall stand in his holy place?'

---

* The *Oriental Chair* was the one used by King Solomon when he presided as Grand Master, which was lost at the destruction of Jerusalem. We learn by a Masonic tradition contained in the lecture of this degree, that "this chair was of massive gold, with cushions fringed with silver; and was large enough to contain *three persons*."

The next Brother replies: 'He that hath clean hands, and a pure heart; who hath not lifted up his soul unto vanity, nor sworn deceitfully.'

Next Brother: 'He shall receive the blessing from the Lord, and righteousness from the God of his salvation.'

Next Brother: 'This is the generation of them that seek him, that seek thy face, O Jacob.'

Next Brother: 'Selah.'

Next brother: 'Lift up your heads, O ye gates,'—(here the golden door is opened),—' and be ye lifted up,'—[here two of the Brethren raise the golden tabernacle by its staves,* about as high as their heads],—'ye everlasting doors, and the King of Glory shall come in.' [Here the Brethren lower the tabernacle.]

Next Brother: 'Who is this King of Glory?'

Next: 'The Lord, strong and mighty, the Lord, mighty in battle.'

Next Brother: 'Lift up your heads, O ye gates, even lift them up,'—(here they again raise the tabernacle),—' ye everlasting doors, and the King of Glory shall come in.'

Next: 'Who is this King of Glory?'

Next Brother: 'The Lord of Hosts, he is the King of Glory.'

The Brethren all together: 'Selah!'

The tabernacle is now replaced on the temple, and the Most Excellent Master proclaims the Lodge open, when the golden door is closed, and the Brethren take their seats. There is solemnity in the ceremony of opening this Lodge, which it is impossible to convey on paper. A reverential awe pervades the breast of every one present, no matter how often he may have assisted in the ceremony.

If a Candidate has been balloted for, and is in waiting, he is conducted into a private room by two Brethren, when a Brother says the following:

'I was glad when they said unto me, Let us go into the house of the Lord.'—(During the time the Brother is repeating these passages, the other Brother is taking the clothing from off the Candidate.)—' Our feet shall stand within thy gates, O Jerusalem. Jerusalem is builded as a city that is compact together; whither the tribes go up, the tribes of the Lord, unto the testimony of Israel, to give thanks unto the name of the Lord. Pray for the Peace of Jerusalem; they shall prosper that love thee. Peace be within thy walls, and prosperity within thy palaces. For my *Brethren* and *companions*' sake, I will now say, Peace be within thee because of the house of the Lord our God, I will seek thy good.'

By this time (as the Brother speaks very slow, making sufficient pauses, be

---

* The ark, while it was ambulatory with the Tabernacle, was carried by *staves* on the shoulders of the Levites. These staves were overlaid with gold, and put through golden rings made for them. PRID., v. I, p. 302.

tween each sentence to give the other Brother time), the Candidate is deprived of all his clothing except his shirt, and in this situation he is conducted into the Lodge, when the Most Excellent Master addresses him as follows:

"Brother A. B.,—You are for the sixth time within the walls of our sacred tabernacle, and it becomes necessary for you to take upon you an Oath, before you can proceed further. 'Who shall ascend into the hill of the Lord? and who shall stand in his holy place? He that hath clean hands, and a pure heart; who hath not lifted up his soul unto vanity, nor sworn deceitfully.'"

The Candidate is then conducted to the altar, caused to kneel on a cushion with both knees, resting his hands on the Bible, the same as in the last degree, except, instead, of permitting the ends of his fore-fingers and thumbs to barely touch each other, they must now be crossed: i. e., the fore-finger of the right-hand, at the first joint, must cross the fore-finger of the left-hand at the first joint—(the joint nearest the nail); and the thumb of the right-hand, at the first joint, must cross the thumb of the left-hand at the first joint; keeping the hands as flat on the book as possible, as in the past degree; and keeping the other three fingers of each hand as close together as he can, and as far as they can be stretched from the two fore-fingers, which are crossed. This forms a figure which is represented on all escutcheons of Royal Arch Masonry. In this situation the M. E. Master administers the following

OATH.

In the name of God, and the Holy Prophets, I solemnly swear, that the secrets connected with the Degree of Most Excellent Master Mason, which I have received, am about to, or shall hereafter receive, I will keep inviolate within my own breast, except I impart them to such as are lawfully entitled to the same. Further, that I will use all amicable means within my power to save a worthy brother of this degree from injury, either from himself or any other person. I also swear that I will not give the *Grand Hailing-sign of distress*, or *words* of a Most Excellent Master, to any being in any known world without first satisfying myself that such a person is as lawfully entitled to the same as I myself am, except in case of great distress. I furthermore swear, in the name of God, and the Holy Prophets, that I will never suffer to be wronged or injured, if within my power to prevent, the wife, sister, mother, or daughter of a Brother of this degree. In the name of God, and the Holy Prophets."

The Oath being finished, the Candidate is ordered to arise, when he is placed in front of the Temple, and the M. E. Master addresses him thus:

"Brother—you again behold the *outward* sanctuary of King Solomon's Temple. May the Lord prepare your heart to feel the beauties within."

The Candidate is here caused to kneel, when the Master opens the golden door, when the inside of the Temple seems as dark as Egypt, the lights having been previously extinguished by a Brother—when the M. E. Master kneels, and proceeds as follows:

"Then said Solomon, The Lord hath said that he would dwell in thick darkness. But I have built an house of habitation for thee, and a place for thy dwelling forever." "And he stood before the altar of the Lord, in the presence of all the congregation of Israel, and spread forth his hands.—(For Solomon had made a brazen scaffold of five cubits long, and five cubits broad, and three cubits high, and had set it in the midst of the court.)—Now then, O Lord God of Israel, let thy word be verified, which thou hast spoken unto thy servant David.—(But will God in very deed dwell with men on earth! Behold, heaven and the heaven of heavens, cannot contain thee; how much less this house which I have builded!)—Then Solomon again spread forth his hands, and said, Let thine eyes, O Lord, be open upon this house day and night, and hearken unto the prayer which thy servant prayeth toward this place."

The Most Excellent Master continues reciting several lengthy passages, which may be found in the Masonic Monitor, from page 148, to 152, which it is useless here to insert, except such particular parts as serve to illustrate this part of the ceremony. He at length arrives at the following passage:

"Now when Solomon had made an end of praying, THE FIRE CAME DOWN FROM HEAVEN,"—here a Brother applies a light to a train prepared for the purpose, unperceived by the Candidate, which instantly begins to illuminate the Temple—and the Master proceeds:)—"and consumed the burnt-offering and the sacrifices; and THE GLORY OF THE LORD FILLED THE HOUSE!"—By this time the Temple is filled with a pure blaze of flaming light, it having been prepared during the day with combustible materials for the purpose. The Most Excellent Master continues: "And the Priests could not enter into the house of the Lord, because the glory of the Lord had filled the Lord's house."

Here the Most Excellent Master and Candidate arise, and walk around to the north side of the temple, when such illuminated figures are presented to their sight as it is impossible here to describe or enumerate.—(The Brethren maintain a profound silence during all this time).—On the south side of the temple are seen brilliant representations of the implements pertaining to the lower degrees of Masonry, together with all the adornments of that side of the original temple at Jerusalem, as described in the Scriptures; with thousands of other brilliancies too numerous even to name, and which seem more of another world than this. On the west side, the setting sun is descending behind the hills, in all the splendor of a meridian noonday, and other curiosities indescribable. Getting round to the north, scarcely a gleam of light penetrates through this side of the temple! This is of Masonic ingenuity, and is well understood by all who have studied well the three first degrees.

In front of the temple, where the golden door opens, which faces the *east*, is seen the reservoir containing the materials which give this brilliant light; and by the time the Candidate arrives in front [the Master explains many of the illuminations as they pass around], this source or fountain head appears partially exhausted,* and the light becomes partially dim, when the Most Excellent Master addresses the Candidate as follows:

'Brother—You discover that the light of Divine love is fading: let the Divine fire of heaven expand your heart, and revive it.'

After a momentary pause, as if waiting for the operation to take effect on the Candidate (who cannot refrain from certain feelings of his inward divinity during this time), the light resumes its former luster—which is done by the hand of a Brother, who governs a *secret spring*, wholly unobserved by the Candidate.

During these ceremonies, which cannot be well described, much less made to appear solemn on paper (but which are in their proper places as solemn and imposing as human ceremonies can be made), the Brethren maintain almost a breathless silence.

The Brethren, being all assembled around the temple, and while the illumination is in its greatest splendor, sing the Most Excellent Master's Song, accompanied with flutes and other instruments of music; at the same time marching round, and yet preserving the oblong square in which they first formed. As this song is in the Mason's Monitor, I shall only insert such parts of it as serve to illustrate this part of the ceremony. Having sung the three first verses, while marching round the temple, the Candidate and Most Excellent Master being now in front of the golden door, they all kneel with their faces toward the temple (which is in their center), and sing the last verse, as follows:

"Almighty Jehovah,
Descend now, and fill
This Lodge with thy glory,
Our hearts with good-will!
Preside at our meetings,
Assist us to find
True pleasure in teaching
Good-will to mankind."

---

* The Jews had a sacred fire which came down from heaven upon their altar of burnt-offerings, which they did there ever after, until the destruction of Jerusalem by the Chaldeans, inextinguishably maintain: and with this fire only were all their sacrifices and oblations made; and Nadab and Abihu were punished with death for offering incense to God with other fire. (See Lightfoot's Temple-service.)

CHORUS.

" Thy wisdom inspired the great institution,
Thy strength shall support it, till nature expire;
And when the creation shall fall into ruin,
Its beauty shall rise, through the midst of the fire."

At this instant the materials are again replenished* by means of the private spring, when a blaze bursts forth, if possible, ten times more brilliant than any preceding it, and by means of a pulley held ready by a Brother, a part of the roof of the temple is raised up, when the blaze flames out with such a vivid brightness, that the Brethren involuntarily cover their eyes with their hands. The blaze sometimes reaches nearly to the ceiling,† and perfumes of the most heavenly fragrance imaginable are emitted, consisting of all the different incenses, and odoriferous drugs that can be procured. In truth, one might easily imagine himself in Elysium.

By degrees the light diminishes in brightness, and the Brethren uncover their faces and rise, when the Most Excellent Master addresses the Candidate:

" Brother—you have seen a faint imitation of 'the fire which cometh down from God out of heaven,' and I beseech you to permit the fire of divine love to burn with equal fervor continually in your own heart. Let your affections and thoughts continually ascend unto the Lord as a sweet-smelling savor, thereby preparing for yourself a crown of glory, eternal in the heavens!"

The Brethren now repeat the first verse of the Most Excellent Master's Song, as follows:

All hail to the morning
That bids us rejoice;
The Temple's completed,
Exalt high each voice;
The *Cap-stone* is finish'd,
Our labor is o'er;
The sound of the gavel
Shall hail us no more."

Here the Key Stone is brought forward by a Brother, and replaced in the Temple between the golden cherubims (it having been removed previously to opening the Lodge), the golden door is closed, and thus closes this part of

---

* The holy fire first descended upon the altar in the tabernacle at the consecrating of Aaron and his sons to the priesthood, and afterward it descended anew upon the altar in the Temple of Solomon, at the consecrating of that Temple. And then it was constantly fed and maintained by the priests, day and night, without even suffering it to go out.

† It is well known that a few years since the Exchange Coffee House was burnt down in Boston, and none but Masons of this degree know to this day the manner in which it caught. It was given out that a party who had been playing cards, had left a candle burning in one of the rooms, by which it was communicated, but the *truth* is, a chapter was held in an upper room, and had arrived at this very crisis in the ceremony of conferring this degree, when the fire first took; so the manner in which it originated no longer remains a mystery.

the ceremony. (I might have previously stated that the insides of the blocks of which the Temple is built, are thoroughly lined with brass or copper plates, to prevent their taking fire.) The M. E. Master now says:

"I shall now present you with the words and signs of this degree. The due-guard sign is given by holding your hands flat before you, thus—letting your right thumb cross your left at the first joint, and your right fore-finger crossing your left at the same; keeping your other three fingers of each hand as far from them as possible. You will then raise them perpendicularly before your face (with their backs almost touching your face), then let them separate and drop by your side with a flap. This is the due-guard sign, and alludes to the situation of your hands when you took the Oath.

"The grand hailing-sign of this degree or sign of distress, is this—(here the Master covers his eyes with his left-hand, with his thumb in a perpendicular position over his left temple)—and has allusion to the way and manner in which you protected your eyes from the bright effulgence, when 'the glory of the Lord filled the house.'—Accompanying this sign, while your eyes are yet covered, in case of great distress you are allowed to pronounce the words, 'AND THE GLORY OF THE LORD FILLED THE HOUSE!' These were the expressions made use of in ancient times, in the Hebrew language; but since Christianity has become established upon the earth, in many Lodges they teach the Candidate the following in lieu thereof: 'ELOI' ELOI! LA MA SABACTHINAI!' or which is the same thing, in English,—'MY GOD, MY GOD, WHY HAST THOU FORSAKEN ME!' Either of these expressions will immediately be recognized if there be a Brother of this degree within hearing, who will instantly fly to your relief. This last sign, and these words, Brother, you will remember you have solemnly sworn to give only to such as are lawfully entitled to the same, except when you are in great distress."

The Candidate is then conducted into the private room, and reclothed. The Most Excellent Master takes his station, and the Brethren are seated. In due time the Candidate is re-introduced, and conducted before the Most Excellent Master in the East, who delivers the following

CHARGE.

'BROTHER: Your admittance to this degree of Masonry, is a proof of the good opinion the Brethren of this Lodge entertain of your Masonic abilities. Let this consideration induce you to be careful of forfeiting, by misconduct and inattention to our rules, that esteem which has raised you to the rank you now possess.

'It is one of your great duties, as a Most Excellent Master, to dispense light and truth to the uninformed Mason; and I need not remind you of the impossibility of complying with this obligation without possessing an accurate acquaintance with the lectures of each degree.

'If you are not already completely conversant in all the degrees heretofore conferred on you, remember, that an indulgence, prompted by a belief that you will apply yourself with double diligence to make yourself so, has induced the Brethren to accept you.

'Let it therefore be your unremitting study to acquire such a degree of knowledge and information as shall enable you to discharge with propriety the various duties incumbent on you, and to preserve unsullied the title now conferred upon you of a Most Excellent Master.'

The Candidate then takes a seat, and the Lodge is closed with nearly the same ceremonies as those performed at opening; which, however unimportant or trifling they may appear on paper, of that sublime and imposing nature which cannot fail to soften, at least for the time, the stoutest heart.

The lecture of this degree will be found very interesting, by such as see proper to visit a Lodge and hear it. The different sections bring to light many matters connected with the completion of the temple at Jerusalem, which have only been preserved from oblivion in the faithful breasts of Most Excellent Masters. Among other things not related in the Scriptures, we learn that at the time ' when Solomon had make an end of praying,' and when *'the fire came down from heaven,'* one of the head workmen of the temple who was present, was so struck with the sublimity of the scene, and his mind being influenced with such a reverential awe, that he was *translated, the same as Elijah!* It may seem strange that his disappearance was not noticed by the surrounding thousands, and the circumstance handed down in the Scriptures; but the probability is that the spectators were so awed by the grandeur of the scene, that they took no note of aught else that transpired. The workmen of the temple all stood in one group, and this Brother was seen to ascend until fairly out of sight.

THE MEANS TO BE USED BY SUCH AS ARE NOT MASONS, TO GAIN ADMISSION INTO ANY LODGE OF MOST EXCELLENT MASTERS ON THE FACE OF THE GLOBE.

The examination at the door of a Most Excellent Master's Lodge is very short, and will soon test the qualifications of a visiting Brother. On making your request known to the Tyler, as in the last degree, two Brothers will be sent out to examine you; and being conducted into the **private room**, you will say—(addressing yourself to one of them—)

'All hail, Most Excellent Masters.'

M. E. Master. All hail.*

---

* Those acquainted with the writings of Shakspeare, will at once discover that he was a Mason. Not only does he show it in Macbeth, but his Hamlet is full of it. *Ghost* "Mark me!" "Safe-bind, Safe-find me," &c.

Applicant. I am a Most Excellent Master Mason, and claim admission into this Lodge.

M. E. Master. Prove yourself such, and yo will be received and acknowledged.

Applicant. What would you have, Brother?

M. E. Master. A sign.

Applicant.—(Here give the *due-guard sign*, by placing your hands flat before you, with their backs up, as when you took the oath; with the right thumb crossing the left at the joint nearest the nail, and the right fore-finger crossing the same joint of the left fore-finger, as explained before; then bring your hands up before your face in this situation, so that your fingers —except the two fore ones—point directly upward; then let them separate and drop by your side, with a flap.)

M. E. Master. What sign is that, Brother?

Applicant. The due-guard sign of a Most Excellent Master.

M. E. Master. When did that sign originate, Brother?

Applicant. When the first Most Excellent Master took his oath.

M. E. Master. To what does it allude, Brother?

Applicant. To the manner in which my hands were placed, when I was qualifying myself to take upon me this degree.

M. E. Master. Have you any other sign, Brother?

Applicant. I have, Most Excellent.

M. E. Master. Give me it, Brother.

Applicant. I cannot, at this time, Most Excellent.

M. E. Master. I am satisfied, Most Excellent Brother, that you are entitled to admission.

You will then be introduced, when you will proceed to the middle of the floor, and give the due-guard sign and take a seat.—*End of the sixth Degree.*

SEVENTH DEGREE OF MASONRY.

THE MODE AND MANNER OF CONFERRING THE DEGREE OF ROYAL ARCH MASON ON A CANDIDATE—IT BEING THE SEVENTH, AND LAST DEGREE OF ANCIENT MASONRY; TOGETHER WITH THE MEANS TO BE USED BY SUCH AS ARE NOT MASONS, TO GAIN ADMISSION INTO ANY CHAPTER OF ROYAL ARCH MASONS ON THE FACE OF THE GLOBE.

"This degree is indescribably more august, sublime, and important than all which precede it; and is the summit and perfection of ancient Masonry. It impresses on our minds a conviction of the being and existence of a **Supreme Deity**, without beginning of days, or end of years; and reminds us of the reverence due to his holy name.

"This degree brings to light many essentials of the Craft, which were for the space of four hundred and seventy years buried in darkness; and without a knowledge of which the Masonic character cannot be complete."

I feel myself more than ever as standing upon "holy ground," now I approach this degree—this *Ne Plus Ultra* of Masonry; and almost incompetent to perform the task before me: yet, if I do not rehearse all the ceremonies introduced in this degree (as I necessarily must not, as they of themselves would fill this work), I shall present the main particulars; and such arcana as will enable any one who chooses to visit any Chapter on the globe, when he can see with his own eyes, and hear with his own ears, the things here related, together with various other matters which are omitted.

The Chapter being assembled, the three head officers take their stations, which are the same as the Master and Wardens in a Lodge. These three officers are, The High Priest, King, and Scribe. The High Priest is clad in a blue robe, and is seated in the East under a canopy, with a scepter in his hand; the King is stationed in the west, and wears a purple robe; and the Scribe in the South, wearing a robe of the deepest scarlet. The Captain of the Host, Principal Sojourner, and other officers, all have clothing peculiar to their stations, and are promiscuously disposed around the Chapter room, when the High Priest recites the following passage:

"Now we command you, Brethren, that ye withdraw yourselves from every Brother that walketh disorderly, and not after the tradition which ye received of us. For yourselves know how ye ought to follow us, for we behaved ourselves not disorderly among you. Neither did we eat any man's bread for naught, but wrought with labor and travel day and night, that we might not be chargeable to any of you. Not because we have not power, but to make ourselves an example unto you to follow us. For even when we were with you, this we commanded you, that if any would not work, neither should he eat; for we hear there are some who walk among you disorderly, working not at all, but are busy-bodies. Now, them that are such, we command and exhort, that with quietness they work, and eat their own bread. But ye, Brethren, be ye not weary in well-doing. And if any man obey not our word, note that man, and have no company with him, that he may be ashamed. Yet count him not as an enemy, but admonish him as a brother. Now, the Lord of peace himself give you peace always. The salutation of Paul, with mine own hand, which is the token; so I write."

Having concluded, the Companions all kneel, when the H. P. proceeds: "Great Architect of the Universe, we again appear in thy holy presence, with a sincere desire that our hearts may be free from guile. Purify, O Lord, our inward tabernacle, and grant that our works may redound to the glory of thy Holy Name." Response: '*So mote it be!*'

The H. P., King and Scribe now descend from their several stations, and approach a *New* Temple which is placed on the middle of the floor, and about four times the size of the one used in the Mark, and M. E. Master's degrees; when the H. P. repeats the following:

"For thus saith the Lord of Hosts, Yet once, it is a little while, and I will shake the heavens, and the earth, and the sea, and the dry land: and I will shake all nations, and the desire of all nations shall come, and I will fill this house with glory. The silver is mine, and the gold is mine.—The glory of this latter house shall be greater than of the former, and in this place will I give peace. Moreover, the word of the Lord came unto me, saying, The hands of Zerubbabel have laid the foundation of this house, his hands shall also finish it; and thou shalt know that the Lord of Hosts hath sent me unto you. For who hath despised the day of small things? for they shall rejoice, and shall see the plummet in the hands of Zerubbabel with those seven." (This is an ancient prophesy, and has allusion to the rebuilding of the second temple, after the destruction of the former one, which is represented to have take place in this degree.)

The Companions now move in solemn procession around the temple, until the H. P. has delivered a lengthy passage from the Scriptures, at the end of which, he proclaims the Chapter open, when the officers take their stations and the Companions their seats.

The Chapter being opened, and a Candidate in waiting, he is conducted into the private apartment by three of the Companions, and divested of all his clothing, save his shirt, when one of them says, "Naked* you came into the world, and naked you must return." He then desires him to take off his shirt, and put on '*The apron of fig-leaves.*'† The apron is lying before the Candidate, and the three Companions having turned their backs, he strips off his shirt and girds on the apron as requested. A pair of Oriental Slippers are then put on his feet, which completes his preparation for this sublime degree.

These slippers are somewhat curious, and as many will read this work who will never visit a Chapter to see them, particularly *females*, I shall attempt a partial description of them. They are woven together without a seam, in

---

* Man, before the transgression, was *naked*, and yet not ashamed. Gen. ii. 25. But after, he knew he was naked. Gen. iii. 7–11. Saul being *naked*, prophesied with the Prophets. 1 Sam xix. 24.

† This apron is composed of real leaves, and is intended to represent the one worn by Adam in the garden of Eden, after he had partaken of the forbidden fruit. It reaches entirely around him, and descends nearly to the knees, so that no very material breach of modesty is made: and yet, what modest *lady* (who is often heard railing against the Masons for their not admitting her sex), would willingly be present at this ceremony; much less, have it performed on herself! In my travels among the Indians, I have seen whole nations duly prepared, in their ordinary dress, to be make Royal Arch Masons, excepting the substitution of cloth or leather, for the leaves of trees.

modern Chapters, from the bark of the elm tree, split to about the size of common stocking yarn. It is presumable that anciently they were manufactured from the bark of the same tree that afforded the wrappers in which Egyptian Mummies were enshrouded and embalmed: but this is more conjecture, although there is no good reason to disbelieve it. The fact that anciently the same tree produced clothing for a Mummy, and slippers for Royal Arch Masons, is further established by the following extract from an ancient work on the "Museum of Antiquities" at Rome:

"On one shelfe in thee corner of this roome layed a show or slippur madde of some verie finne barkk of tree, which was verie and extreemlie finne, and madde entyrelie wholle without seame or linning, and was wraughte verie curiouslie and witth mutch ingenuousnesse. They sayed ytt had belonnged ancientlie to somme King who had been slayne in battel, and was of sutch texture as formerlie they wraughte to enshroude sutch menne of greate valyor that ytt was deemed meete to imbamme in theire tommbes," &c.

These slippers are much longer than the feet, and are peaked at the toes. The heel of each forms two right angles of a square, and is not circular, as other shoes. They are ornamented all over so as partially to resemble the Indian Moccasins, which are decorated with quills of the porcupine, but with this difference: the slippers used in a chapter are ornamented with gold and silver tinsel, forming the ancient hieroglyphics of the Egyptians, which some pretend to understand and explain; whereas the Indian moccasin is merely ornamented in the ordinary drapery style. But to our subject.

During the time the Candidate is in preparation, the companions within the Chapter prepare the room for his reception in a manner which will be seen after his introduction. All things being in readiness, he is taken in by the three companions, when the first thing that meets his eye is a large Arch situated directly over the temple,* and reaching nearly to the ceiling. (This arch is composed of several pieces, which are kept in a large chest under lock and key, that they may not be seen by Brethren of a lower degree; and when used in the Chapter, are fastened together with screws.)

In the center of this arch, i. e. where the key stone is usually placed, it is discovered that the key stone is gone, and consequently the arch meets together in such a manner as to make it irregular. The Candidate is then, by means of a ladder of seven rounds, conducted up to the center of the arch, which is opened, and he is placed in the opening instead of the key stone, with his face fronting the East,† and his arms extended along over the arch

---

* This temple is about four times as large as the one used in other degrees, and is capable of containing five or six persons.

† Speaking of the mode of worship taught by Zoroaster and his disciples, H. Prideaux, p. 389, says, "But this was not a new institution of his: We find in Ezekiel, v. 16, where it is related, that the prophet being carried in a vision to Jerusalem, saw, among other things, 'about five and twenty men standing between the porch and the

in opposite directions. (The two ends of the arch, at the opening, come close under his arms, which gives the appearance that the arch is whole, and passes directly through his body.) His feet are permitted to rest on the roof of the temple beneath, although I have known very short men compelled to support themselves, during the whole ceremony, by their arms resting on the arch. This was the intention and custom, originally, but for several centuries past it has been found so very severe on the Candidate, that the other mode has been adopted. Its intention was to teach those who should be exalted to this degree, "patience and long suffering" in the cause of truth. When a very short man takes this degree, blocks are furnished for his feet to rest upon, but this practice was unknown in ancient times; and many enlightened Masons question the propriety of it in our days.

In this situation, the High Priest addresses the Candidate as follows:

" MOST EXCELLENT BROTHER—You are now placed in the situation in which all Royal Arch Masons have been placed, previous to receiving this sublime degree."

The H. Priest then administers the following

AFFIRMATION.*

"In the name of the EVERLASTING GOD, the Holy Prophets and Evangelists, I do most solemnly affirm, that the degree of Royal Arch Mason, or any part thereof, shall never be communicated by me to any person or persons in any known world, except to such as have taken upon themselves the degress of Entered Apprentice, Fellow-Craft, Master, Mark-Master, Past-Master, Most Excellent Master, and Royal Arch Mason (except I am presiding as High Priest over a Chapter, in which case the last named degree is excepted); and not to those even until I am fully satisfied within my own mind that they have legally and lawfully received the same. I also solemnly affirm, that I will use my utmost endeavors to preserve peace and harmony among my companions of this degree, when in the Chapter, as well as when associated with the world: that I will not injure, or suffer to be injured in any manner, a companion of this degree, if within my knowledge and power to prevent: that the widows and orphans of companions of this degree, shall receive my protection and support, as far as in my power lies, the same as those of my own blood. Furthermore do I most solemnly affirm, that I will

---

altar, *with their faces toward the east.*'—For the Holy of holies [in which was the *Shechinah* of the divine presence resting over the mercy-seat and cherubims], being on the western end of the Temple at Jerusalem, all that entered thither to worship God, did it with their faces turned that way, i. e. toward the east; for that was their **Kebla** or the point toward which they always directed their worship."

* No Royal Arch-Mason is allowed to swear, either in the Chapter or a Court of Justice.

not give the Grand Hailing-Sign and Words of a Royal Arch Mason, or any or either of them, except when in danger of my life, nor then, except I have substantial reasons to believe a Royal Arch Mason is within hail, who can save it. Furthermore, that in my intercourse with my Fellow-men, I will be upright and just, and never be guilty of any act which shall sully the dignity of my profession, or forfeit the respect and veneration due to this sublime Institution. In the name of the Everlasting God, the Holy Prophets and Evangelists."

This constitutes the affirmation of a Royal Arch Mason. The High Priest now recites the following:

"Supreme Architect of Universal Nature, who, by thine almighty word, didst speak into being the stupendous Arch of Heaven, and, for the instruction and pleasure of thy rational creatures, didst adorn us with greater and lesser lights; thereby magnifying thy power, and endearing thy goodness unto the sons of men: we humbly adore and worship thine unspeakable perfection. We bless thee that when man had fallen from his innocence and his happiness, thou didst still leave unto him the power of reasoning, and capacity of improvement and pleasure. We thank thee that amidst the pains and calamities of our present state, so many means of refreshment and satisfaction are reserved unto us, while traveling the *rugged path of life* Especially would we at this time render thee our thanksgiving and praise for the institution, as members of which we are at this time assembled, and for all the pleasures we have derived from it. We thank·thee that the few here assembled before thee, have been favored with new inducements, and laid under new and stronger obligations, to virtue and holiness. May these obligations, Oh blessed Father, have their full effect upon us. Teach us, we pray thee, the true reverence of thy great, mighty, and terrible name. Inspire us with a firm and unshaken resolution in our virtuous pursuits. Give us grace diligently to search thy word in the Book of Nature, wherein the duties of our high vocation are inculcated with divine authority. May the solemnity of the ceremonies of our institution be duly impressed on our minds, and have a lasting and happy effect upon our lives. May all thy *miracles and mighty works* fill us with the dread, and thy goodness impress us with the love, of thy holy name. May *holiness to the Lord* be engraved on all our thoughts, words, and actions. May the increase of piety ascend continually unto thee from the *altar* of our hearts, and burn, day and night, as a sacrifice of a sweet-smelling savor, well pleasing unto thee. And since sin has destroyed within us the *first temple* of purity and innocence, may thy heavenly grace guide and assist us in rebuilding a *second temple* of reformation, and may the glory of this latter hour be greater than the glory of the former. *Amen.*"

Response: "*So mote it be!*"

The center pieces of the arch on which the arms of the Candidate are resting, are now removed, and the Candidate is told to *suffer his arms to make their own motion;* and as the center pieces are both removed at the same time, his arms, of course, drop by his sides with a flap; and this is the due-guard sign of a Royal Arch Mason. Perhaps this is the most proper time to instruct the reader in this due-guard sign: You will extend your arms in about the same direction from your body as though you had a *barrel* under each, though not suffer your fingers to point quite so much toward your body as you would in that case;—then bring them down with a *flap* to your sides. This is the due-guard sign of this degree, and alludes to the situation of your hands and arms, when you took upon yourself the affirmation of a Royal Arch Mason; which was, *with your arms extended from the center of the arch, toward its base,* in a circular direction. It will be seen that if the arms were not attached to the shoulders, but passed directly through them and joined in the middle, a perfect arch would be formed. Care must be taken to prevent any sudden bend in the elbows, but let them form a gentle curve, so as to resemble, as much as possible, an arch.

The Candidate is now standing on the top of the temple, and the Royal Arch is removed a foot or two back to give him ample room, when the High Priest recites the following passage:

"I will bring the blind by a way that they know not; I will lead them in paths that they have not known; I will make the darkness light before them, and crooked things straight: These things will I do unto them, and will not forsake them."

Here the High Priest descends from his station, and approaches the temple, when by means of the ladder of *seven rounds,* he ascends and stands by the side of the Candidate;* when he opens a trap door which the Candidate has not before discovered, and descends, desiring him to follow. Being now within the temple, and the trap door closed over their heads, the High Priest proceeds as follows:

"And when the Lord saw that he turned aside to see, God called unto him, *out of the midst of the bush,* and said,—here a companion *without* the temple says, 'Moses, Moses!'—when the High Priest answers, 'Here am I.' The High Priest continues: 'And he said,'—here the companion without says, 'draw not nigh hither: *Put off thy shoes from off thy feet, for the place whereon thou standest is holy ground.*' Here the High Priest takes off his shoes,† and teaches the Candidate to do the same. The High Priest continues: 'Moreover he said,'—here the companion without (who is the captain of the host), says, 'I am the God of thy father, the God of Abraham, the God of Isaac, and the God of Jacob,' The High Priest now says,—'and Moses hid his face, for he was afraid to look upon God.'—(Here they hide their

---

* *Three* generally take this degree on the same evening, but this part of the ceremony is never performed on more than one at a time

† *Shilo,* or *Shiloh,*—(Hebrew), putting off one's shoes.

faces with their hands, and then withdraw them again.) They now seat themselves on stools with cushions fringed with gold, when the High Priest addresses the Candidate as follows:

"Most Excellent Brother—You have now arrived within the temple of the living God. Let us bow down our faces to the ground and worship the Lord, who is strong and mighty." (Here they bow their faces to the ground.) "O thou who didst aforetime appear unto thy servant Moses *in a flame of fire out of the midst of a bush*, enkindle, we beseech thee, in each of our hearts, a flame of devotion to thee, of love to each other, and of charity to all mankind."

(I should have previously stated, that after the trap door is closed over their heads, the only light admitted within the temple is through a transparency on the east side, resembling the rising sun; but as this is only admitted through oiled paper, it affords but a dim light, and gives everything around them a gloomy and confused appearance: yet, if there is solemnity in any human ceremony, there is in this.)

They now lift their faces from the ground, and are again seated. The High Priest continues: "I now, Most Excellent Brother, withdraw the first vail!" (Hereupon he pulls a cord, and the outward porch of King Solomon's Temple is presented to their view, most brilliantly illuminated,-with the various Masonic implements used in the first degree; rough and perfect ashlers, squares and compasses, twenty-four inch gauges, common gavels, Entered Apprentices at their labor, &c. &c., when the Master of the first vail speaks from without, yet through a tube, which makes his voice sound within the first vail:—"Son of man, mark well the entering in of the gate!" Hereupon the High Priest pulls another cord, which raises the second vail, when all the paraphernalia pertaining to the second and third degrees, appear in the most brilliant colors. The various orders of architecture, as explained in the Fellow Craft's degree; all the emblems which adorn a Master's carpet; Master-Masons at their labors, &c., with thousands of other illuminations of the most brilliant colors, and variegated hues. Here will be one which vies in its vivid blue with the freshest violet; and perhaps adjoining to it, another which might dispute superiority with the lily, in its bright scarlet. But it is impossible to do justice to this part of the subject. One part, however, must not be omitted.

In the center, through a long perspective view of the middle chamber beyond it, however), is seen the *Sanctum Sanctorum*, or *Holy of Holies*. King Hiram is seen lying prostrate on the floor, surrounded by several of his Brethren, weeping. A coffin lies by his side, with the circle of letters on it, as explained in the Mark degree. On the right, a large pedestal, or rather monument, with the words 'VIRTUE AND INTEGRITY' on its front; and on the left, *death's skull and cross-bones*, with a bright flower flourishing directly over it. But I find these things cannot be intelligibly conveyed on paper.

H

After they have viewed these transparencies a few moments, the Master of the second vail speaks through a tube, "Imitate the virtues of departed Innocence!"—The High Priest here withdraws the third and last vail; and here I feel myself wholly incompetent to convey even a faint idea of the beauties presented to view: I shall attempt, however, the more important.

In the center of the panorama, is a magnificent Royal Arch, illuminated with all the variegated hues which human ingenuity can invent. Thousands of small glass lamps, of all colors imaginable, are suspended on either side from the center. The blaze is so dazzling, that the eyes have often been injured to that degree, as to render it necessary to wear goggles after viewing it. In the center of this arch is seen a human being, in the same situation the Candidate was placed a short time before; and the surrounding brilliancies give a lustre to the whole scene, too vivid for the mortal eye to behold. By machinery prepared by ingenious Masons, the man in the center of the arch is seen gradually to ascend, and a proper Key Stone takes his place, and appears firmly fixed. On the stone are the circular letters, and as the man ascends to give it room, he is distinctly heard to say, "He That Was Slain Soars To Kindred Spirits;" but in fact, these expressions are made by the Master of the third vail, through the tube; but the illusion is so complete, that one can imagine he sees the lips move.

Satisfied as I am that I have presented but a very imperfect picture of this part of the ceremony, I shall willingly withdraw from this "holy gound." The High Priest now drops the scene, and the same glimmering sun entering on the east side, is the only light they receive. The High Priest now ascends the ladder of the seven rounds (which was taken from the outside and placed down through the trap door, before they descended), desiring the Candidate to follow; and in a few minutes, having put on their shoes and slippers, they are again standing on the top of the temple, surrounded by all the companions present. This seems to the Candidate like emerging from a world of spirits into a world of mortals; and in truth the sudden transition is such as to make an impression on the mind which can never be removed.

The Candidate is again exalted to his station in the Arch,* with his face toward the east, when the High Priest withdraws the Ladder, and placing it on the outside of the temple, descends, and proceeds to his station in the east, when he addresses the Candidate as follows:

"Most Excellent Brother—-You are now entitled to a full explanation of all the arcana upon which this degree is founded. We learn by a Masonic tradition that at the time Adam was created from the dust, on the very day of his creation, as he was seated on a little eminence under the shade of a

---

* A very beautiful representation of the Candidate in his present situation in the arch, executed by a skillful engraver, has been placed as a frontispiece in the "Masonic Minstrel," and may there be seen. The engraver has, for obvious reasons, omitted to place his arms in their proper situation

fig-tree, an angel appeared before him with a scroll in his right-hand, and addressed Adam as follows, in the Hebrew language: 'Lo, Man, beware of the temptation which will be offered unto thee. I am sent by thy Maker to warn thee from the death to which thou wilt be exposed shouldst thou listen to other counsel than that which the Lord thy God hath implanted within thine own bosom: beware, therefore, of temptation. Lo, Man! Look upon this!' Here the angel unrolled the scroll, which contained Hebrew characters answering to these in our language."

Here the High Priest unrolls a scroll (which he takes from a box which has the appearance of gold, with some Hebrew characters on it), when the Candidate discovers, in large letters—"LORD EVERLASTING, EVERLASTING LORD!"*—The High Priest continues: "These, companion, are the words of a Royal Arch Mason, which you have solemnly affirmed never to utter, save when your life is in imminent danger, nor then, unless you have substantial reasons to believe a companion is within hail, who can save it. The sign accompanying these expressions, you will receive in due-time."

The High Priest now wraps up the scroll, replaces it in the box, and continues:

"Having said this, the angel presented the scroll to Adam, and disappeared from his sight. After the creation of Eve, Adam related unto her the circumstance of the angel, and showed her the scroll; but Eve would not hearken unto his counsel. She partook of the forbidden fruit, and did eat, and through her entreaties, Adam also. After this they were ashamed, and clothed themselves in aprons of fig-leaves, gathered from the very tree under which Adam sat when the angel appeared unto him. You are thus clad this evening, companion, the better to impress upon your mind the warning given by the angel unto Adam; and now, in the language of the Angel, I caution thee to *beware of all temptations which will be presented unto thee*, in all thy travels through the *rugged paths* of life."

Here the High Priest descends, and proceeds to the temple, which he ascends by the ladder of seven rounds, and continues:

"And by obedience to this warning voice, may you prepare for yourself a CROWN OF GLORY in the heavens, transcending in brilliant diadems the one which I now present you, as spiritual things transcend material."

Here a companion presents to the High Priest a splendid crown, encircled around with 'HOLINESS TO THE LORD,' which he places on the head of the newly-exalted companion, when all present exclaim, '*Holiness to the Lord!*' The High Priest then continues the tradition:

---

* In Jewish Chapters these words are given in the Hebrew language: "ADONAI OULEM, OULEM ADONAI." It will be discovered that these words read the same backward and forward, in accordance with many passages in the Scriptures which declare the Lord is, 'without beginning or ending,' 'the first and the last,' 'the Alpha and Omega,' 'without turning, or the shadow of a change,' &c.

"This scroll, which the angel gave unto Adam, was handed down from father to son, until the building of the Temple by Solomon, and was by him used when this degree was conferred, to teach Candidates the words of this degree, which were first given by the Lord to Adam, through the angel. As these words could not be uttered except when life was endangered, and as no part of them could be written or engraved, upon anything movable or immovable,* this was the only instrument by which they could be taught. This scroll was always intrusted to the care of Hiram Abbiff, who so well knew the importance of his charge, that, unknown to Solomon, or any other person, he caused a deep vault to be made under the southernmost part of the temple, and so completely arched over and covered, that the most penetrating eye could not discover it. To effect this, he procured laborers from a foreign country, and bound them by a Solemn Oath never to divulge it. The entrance to this vault was through the wall of the room wherein King Hiram formed his designs, previous to laying them down on the Trestle-board; and the door of the entrance was so nicely contrived, that no human eye could notice any difference in the wall; and it never was discovered unto this day.†

"In this vault King Hiram deposited this scroll, and never removed it except on occasions like the present. After the death of this worthy Brother, in the melancholy manner related in the third degree, these words were lost and were nowhere to be found. Strict search was made in the most secret recesses of the *sanctum sanctorum*, all to no purpose. The sudden death of Hiram was a sad blow to Masonry. This scroll lay buried in darkness in this vault for the space of *four hundred and seventy years* during which period Royal Arch Masonry may be said to have slept.

"Sometime after the rebuilding of the second temple by Zerubbabel and his Companions, this vault and this scroll were discovered in the following singular manner:

"A Lodge of Master-Masons was sitting in a lower room of the temple directly over this vault,‡ the floor of which, near the south-west corner, was somewhat decayed; and by some accident a Brother stepped on a plank which partially gave way; and in saving himself, his *trowel* dropped

---

* See Entered Apprentice's Obligation in "Jachin and Boaz."

† HUMPHREY PRIDEAUX, in his researches, certainly gained *some* knowledge of this ark, though not the true, as he imputes to Solomon and King Josiah that which belongs to Hiram Abbiff. Witness the following: "But most of them will have it, that King Josiah, being foretold by Huldah the prophetess, that the temple would speedily after his death be destroyed, caused the ark to be put in a vault under ground, which Solomon, foreseeing this destruction, had caused of purpose to be built, for the preserving of it, in which vault, they say, it hath lain hid ever since, even to this day."—Vol. 1, pp. 303-4.

‡ But this is not to be understood of its bigness: for the second temple was of the same dimensions with the first; *it being built upon the very same foundations*. Con. O O. & N. Test., H. Prideaux, v. 1, p. 294.

through the opening on the ground underneath the floor. The High Priest now recites the following passages:

"For there was a tabernacle made; the first, wherein was the candlestick, and the table, and the shew-bread; which is called the sanctuary. And after the vails, the tabernacle, which is called, The Holiest of all; which had the golden censer, and the ark of the covenant overlaid roundabout with gold, wherein was the golden pot that had manna, and Aaron's rod that budded, and the tables of the covenant; and over it the cherubims of glory, shadowing the mercy-seat; of which we cannot now speak particularly."

"In that day will I raise up the tabernacle of David *that is fallen* and *close up the breaches* thereof, and I will *raise up* his ruins, and I will build it as in the days of old.'

" 'In the beginning was the word, and the word was with God, and the word was God.'" After reciting these passages from scripture, the High Priest proceeds with the tradition:

"This accident causing a slight interruption in their labors, a part of the flooring was removed, when the Brother stepped down on the ground to reach his trowel, when it gave way beneath his feet, and he was precipitated to the bottom of the vault, a distance of full fifteen feet! A ladder was now provided, and eight other Brethren descended with lights, when it was found that the Brother who had fallen through the decayed arch, had received a serious fracture in the fall, on the top of his head; and having his hands clasped together by the fingers, was pressing them on the fracture to prevent the effusion of blood. He pressed them on so hard that it was with difficulty the Brethren could remove them. On examining the apartment, a box was found of pure gold, firmly locked, with the key-hole in the exact form of the letter G, and on the top was engraved 'HIRAM ABBIFF—SACRED.' The Brethren immediately recollected that a key in form of the letter G had been preserved in the archives of the Lodge from time immemorial, and none of them had known the use of it; and on calling to their Brethren above, it was thrown down to them, when they easily unlocked their treasure, and to their great joy found the long lost scroll, containing the sacred words: and before ascending they agreed that the Grand hailing-sign of this degree, should thereafter be the one made by the Brother who had received the injury; and should only be given when life was in danger; nor then unless there was a prospect that it might thereby be preserved.

"This sign is given by shoving all the fingers of each hand between each other lengthwise, keeping the hands flat with the backs up, and each thumb pointing directly toward your body; and then raise them in this situation very slowly, considerably above your head (directly over it), so as to form an arch; then bring them down on the top of your head, pressing down heavy on it, at the same time pulling slowly, so as in a short time to let the fingers slip from between each other, and your arms and hands drop down by your side with a flap. This sign, Companion, is the Grand hailing-sign of this degree, and can only be given as agreed on by the nine Brethren in the vault, when it may be accompanied by the words on the scroll.

"After forming this agreement, the nine Brethren ascended the ladder, and, acquainting the rest of the Brethren of their discoveries, they all entered into a solemn contract to conform to it. The name of the Brother who received the injury (of which he shortly recovered), was *Nebat*, who was ever after complimented by his Brethren for having dropped his trowel through the crevice in the floor, as it had been the means of restoring to the Masonic fraternity that which might otherwise have remained in darkness forever.

"I have further to inform you, Companion, that the key of this golden tabernacle, which was in the form of the letter G, our Grand Master, Hiram Abbiff, ever carried in a pocket near his left breast—and near his heart. Thus he carried it, when he was slain by the ruffians, and falling on his left side, it made the faint impression which was discovered on that part of his body after it was found. After the ruffians had slain him, they searched his body, and took from his pocket this key; but not knowing the use of it, they threw it among the clefts of the rocks at the time they were detected and taken, where it was found a short time after by some Master-Masons who were examining the spot—who also not knowing the use of it, it was laid up in the archives of the Lodge by order of King Solomon, where it had remained useless until the period when the discovery was accidentally made which I have just related to you. You are now made acquainted with the principal ground-work of this degree; but in the LECTURE you will discover innumerable beauties which cannot be made to appear at this time.

"You are now, Companion, exalted to the sublime degree of Royal Arch Mason."

The Candidate is now taken down from the arch, and conducted to the private room and reclothed, and then conveyed before the High Priest in the East, who gives him the following

CHARGE.

"WORTHY COMPANION: By the consent and assistance of the members of this Chapter, you are now exalted to the sublime and honorable degree of a Royal Arch Mason.

"Having attained this degree, you have arrived at the summit and perfection of ancient Masonry; and are consequently entitled to a full explanation of the mysteries of the order.

"The rites and mysteries developed in this degree have been handed down through a chosen few, unchanged by time, and uncontrolled by prejudice:

and we expect and trust, they will be regarded by you with the same veneration, and transmitted with the same scrupulous purity to your successors.

"No one can reflect on the ceremonies of gaining admission into this place, without being forcibly struck with the important lessons which they teach.

" Here we are necessarily led to contemplate with gratitude and admiration the sacred source from whence all earthly comforts flow; here we find additional inducements to continue steadfast and immovable in the discharge of our respective duties; and here we are bound, by the most solemn ties, to promote each other's wellfare, and correct each other's failings, by advice, admonition and reproof.

"As it is our most earnest desire, and a duty we owe to our Companions of this order, that the admission of every Candidate into this Chapter shall be attended by the approbation of the most scrutinizing eye, we hope always to possess the satisfaction of finding none amongst us, but such as will promote to the utmost of their power the great end of our institution. By paying due attention to this determination, we expect you will never recommend any Candidate to this Chapter, whose abilities and knowledge of the foregoing degrees, you cannot freely vouch for, and whom you do not firmly and confidently believe, will fully conform to the principles of our order, and fulfill the obligations of a Royal Arch Mason. While such are our members, we may expect to be united in one object, without lukewarmness, inattention or neglect; but zeal, fidelity, and affection, will be the distinguishing characteristics of our society, and that satisfaction, harmony and peace may be enjoyed at our meetings, which no other society can afford."

The Chapter is then closed with similar ceremonies to those used at opening, which it is useless here to recapitulate. Were I to insert all the ceremonies and passages practiced and read during the conferring of this degree, they of themselves would fill a book considerably larger than the New Testament—as any one may discover who will visit a Chapter, and remain present during the conferring of this degree.

The Chapter being closed with solemn ceremonies, the following prayer is rehearsed by the Most Excellent High Priest:

"By the *Wisdom* of the Supreme High Priest may we be directed, by his *Strength* may we be enabled, and by the *Beauty* of virtue may we be incited, to perform the obligations here enjoined on us: to keep inviolably the mysteries here unfolded to us, and invariably to practice all those duties *out* of the Chapter, which are inculcated *in* it."

Response: '*So mote it be!*' '*Amen.*'

The Companions then disperse, and the Captain of the Host sees that the Temple, Royal Arch, &c. are properly disposed of; and thus concludes the ceremony of conferring this degree

THE MEANS TO BE USED BY SUCH AS ARE NOT MASONS, TO GAIN ADMISSION INTO ANY CHAPTER OF ROYAL ARCH MASONS ON THE FACE OF THE GLOBE.

In this degree it is seldom that more is required of a visitor, than barely the due-guard sign, as it is so utterly impossible that any one not having taken this degree should be in the possession of it; but sometimes a stranger who claims admission is taken into the private room, and undergoes the following examination:

Applicant. I claim admission into this Chapter of Royal Arch Masons.

R. A. Mason. By what rights do you claim admission?

Applicant. By the rights of the Royal Arch. [Here give the due-guard sign as directed in page 116.]

R. A. Mason. To what does that allude?

Applicant. To my situation in the Royal Arch, when I was exalted to this degree.

R. A. Mason. I am satisfied, Most Excellent Companion, that your claims to admission into our Holy Sanctuary are well founded.

You will then be introduced, when, as in the preceding degrees, you will proceed to the center of the floor, give the due-guard sign, and then take a seat.—*End of the Seventh, and last Degree of Ancient Masonry.*

RECAPITULATION.

I SHALL now recapitulate the Due-Guard Signs, Grand Hailing-Signs of Distress, Words, Words of Distress, &c. of the several degrees; which will give the reader a more condensed view of the necessary prerequisites to his gaining admission into Chapters and Lodges.

A MARK-MASTER places his hands behind him, with the backs together, and brings them round together in front, crossing each other (the right one uppermost), with a loud clap, four times in succession. This is called the *Mark Master's Due-Guard Sign and Clap*. The Grand Hailing-Sign of this Degree, or Sign of Distress is made by raising the right arm in a horizontal position, pointing forward with the fore-finger (the rest being closed), and forming in the air the letter K, with a period, or dot after it, and then letting the arm drop by the side with a flap; again raise the arm, and form in the air the letter S, with a period, or dot after it, and then suffer the arm to drop by the side with a flap, as before. The GRIP of a Mark-Master is given by pressing the thumb-nail into the upper joint, or last joint from the nail, of the third finger of the right hand. Its name is CHAOS.

A PAST-MASTER places his hands flat before him, with the backs up, suffering the ends of his two fore-fingers and thumbs to meet so as to form a triangle; then raises them to his face so as to look through the two lower angles, and in a few seconds lets them part, and drop by each hip with a flap. The words accompanying this sign (on proper occasions), are TRIANGLE OF TRUTH. There was no Grip to this degree, anciently, but some modern Past-Masters press the thumb between the third and little finger of the right hand, and call it the *pass* or *past*-Grip of this degree; and then passing the thumb along to the upper joint of the little finger, press in the nail, and call it the *Grip* of a Past-Master, and give it the name of *Chibbilum*, which name, they say, signifies *Triangle*.

A MOST EXCELLENT MASTER places his hands flat before him, with the backs up, with the right thumb crossing the left thumb at the joint, and the right fore-finger crossing the left fore-finger at the first joint, the other fingers of each hand stretched as far as possible from each fore-finger; he then raises them in this situation in front of his face, and then lets them separate and drop by his side with a flap. This is the *Due-Guard Sign* of a Most Excellent Master. The Grand Hailing-Sign of this degree, or Sign of Distress, is given by covering the eyes with the left-hand, the thumb pointing in a perpendicular direction, and reaching along over the left temple. The words accompanying this sign (on proper occasions), **or words of distress,** are these: "AND THE GLORY OF THE LORD FILLED THE HOUSE;" or, "ELOI! ELOI! LA MA SABACTHANAI!" or, "MY GOD! MY GOD! WHY HAST THOU FORSAKEN ME!"

A ROYAL ARCH MASON raises his arms as if he held a barrel under each arm, and brings them down on each side, with a flap. This is called the *Due-Guard Sign* of a Royal Arch Mason. The Grand Hailing-Sign of this degree, or Sign of Distress, is given as follows: hold your hands before you with their backs up, with the fingers pointing toward each other, and each thumb pointing toward your body; then shove the fingers of each hand between each other, so as to make them firmly interwoven together; in this situation raise them slowly over your head, so that the arms thus joined together by the hands, resemble an arch; then bring the hands (yet joined) down on the top of the head, pressing down hard on the same, and at the same time pulling with each hand, and in a few seconds permit the fingers to slip from between each other, and let your hands drop down by your side with a flap. This is the Grand Hailing-Sign of a Royal Arch Mason, or Sign of Distress; and the words of distress accompanying it (only spoken when life is in danger), are "LORD EVERLASTING, EVERLASTING LORD!" or, in the Hebrew language, "ADONAI OULEM, OULEM ADONAI!"

APPENDIX.

The outer wall of King Solomon's Temple, was a square of five hundred cubits on every side, *i. e.* two thousand in the whole circuit. It was twenty-five cubits high, measuring on the inside, which was the size of all the other, walls of the temple, as well in the inner part as the outer, excepting only that of the *Chel;* every cubit was a foot and a half. The east gate of the temple wall was called *Shusham,* on either side of which, within, was a shop, or repository, for the wine, oil, salt, meal, and other things used in the sacrifices; with chambers over on either side. Between this gate and the western corner, upon a jutting out of the mountain, stood the castle *Antonia,* formerly called *Baris,* where the *Romans* kept garrison to overawe the temple; from hence the captain of it was called the captain of the temple. (See Luke, ch. xxii, v. 52, and Acts, ch. iv, v. 1.) It was a square pile two furlongs in compass, standing at a little distance from the temple wall, and from which there was a passage by stairs down into the cloisters at the north-west corner, through which the soldiers ran down to appease the tumult risen about Paul. (See Acts, ch. xxi, v. 32, and Paul's speech to the people, same ch., v. 40.) There were two gates on the south side of the wall, called the gates of *Huldah,* with the porters' lodge or chamber over each. On the west side were the gates *Challecheth,* or *Coponius,* and *Parbor,* with the porters' lodge or chamber over the same, two gates on either side. Also on the west side, the two gates of *Asuppim,* over each of which a room on either side where a treasury of the temple was kept; the pile of each gate was fifteen cubits broad and thirty high, and the entrance ten cubits broad and twenty cubits high: and all the gates, as well in the inner parts of the temple as the outer, were every one of them of the same size. The portico on the south side of the temple was called the Royal portico, because of its largeness, for it contained three aisles; the middle forty-two cubits and a half broad, and fifty cubits high; the other two, each fifty cubits broad, and twenty-five cubits high, which was the size of all the other porticos of this court. That on the east side was called *Solomon's* porch, because it stood upon that vast terrace which Solomon built up from the valley beneath, of four hundred cubits hight, which was the only work of *Solomon's* temple that remained in our Saviour's time, and therefore it was called *Solomon's* porch, or cloister. (See John, ch. x, v. 23; also Acts, ch. iii, v. 11.) The outer court of the temple was the court of the *Gentiles,* the outer enclosure of the inner court, being a wall curiously wrought, of three cubits hight, within which no Gentile was to enter, or any polluted with the dead. The space between the walls of the outer and inner courts of the temple, was ten cubits broad, and this was called the *Chel*. The stairs on the east end leading from the court of the Gentiles into the *Chel*, consisted of fourteen steps, each nine inches high. The stairs from the *Chel* into the court of the women, consisted of five steps, each nine inches high. The gate entering into the court of the women on the east, was called the Beautiful Gate of the temple, because of its sumptuousness and adornments. (See Acts, ch. iii, v. 2.) The outer gates led to the court of the women—one on the south, the other on the north. The court of the women was so called, because thus far the women might enter to worship, but no further. This court was one hundred and thirty-five cubits square. There were also porticos around the court of the women, over which were galleries for the women. Under the floor of the court of *Israel*, were two rooms where the musicians did lay up their instruments. One room called *Gazeth*, was where the *Sanhedrim* sat, part of which was within the sanctuary, and part without. There was also a well room, where there was a well from whence water was drawn for the use of the temple. Three gates leading into the sanctuary on the south side; the first next the draw-well room was from thence called the well-gate, over which was the room of *Aslines*, where the incense was made; the second was the gate of *Firstlings*, and the third, the gate of *Kindlings*. There was also a common fire-room and chief guard-room for the priests, with a *Stone* in the middle of said room, under which the Keys of the temple were laid every night. There was a room where the lambs were kept for the daily sacrifices, and their skins were dressed to make aprons for the Masons. The stairs up into the porch were twelve in number. The entrance into the porch, twenty cubits broad and forty high. The two pillars, *Jachin* and *Boaz*, stood in the entrance on either side. The holy place was twenty cubits broad, and forty long. The Holy of Holies, twenty cubits square, containing the ark of the covenant, with the two *Cherubims*, each ten cubits high, with their faces inwards, and their wings extended to each other over the ark, and to the walls on each side; the vail of the temple parting between the holy, and the Holy of Holies, which was rent in pieces at our Saviour's death. The length of the temple from out to out, was one hundred cubits. The highest wing of the temple was one hundred and twenty cubits, at the top of which it was that the devil did set our Saviour. (Matt. ch. iv, v. 5.) *These particulars are related according to the Scriptures, Josephus, and the Talmud*, by H. PRIDEAUX, *D. D., Dean of Norwich.*

EXPLANATION.

Having thus completed this Key, &c., I may now be allowed to say a few words in extenuation of conduct which must appear of the basest and blackest character, to every man of any sensibility, and to Royal Arch Masons in particular. The latter, I am aware, will never forgive me; but *all* who do not belong to the institution, be they ever so scrupulous of their *word* and yet a hundred times more scrupulous of their oath, will frankly and cordially acknowledge that I have done no wrong, when they shall *know all*. I have no doubt but the reader has pronounced me a perjured wretch, more than once, while perusing these pages; but *not quite so fast*—hear the sequel.

I have said, "In this degree, it is seldom that more is required of a visitor than the due-guard sign, as it is so utterly impossible that any one not having taken this degree, should be in the possession of it."

This is all very true; and it is to this fact that the reader is indebted for the pages now before him: for were Royal Arch Masons as scrutinizing in their examination of strangers, as *they* are in the three first degrees, these illustrations could never have been presented to the public; as it cannot be supposed, any being could be found sufficiently base to violate oaths of the most sacred nature,—much less could such a being be found within the vail of the Masonic sanctuary.

Several years since, a person in Boston, *not a Mason*, chanced to see one, whom he knew to be a Royal Arch Mason, give the due-guard sign, explained in this degree, to another person. This Mason, having given the sign, turned round and discovered that he had been seen by one not a Mason, and seeming much confused and embarrassed, fell to making all manner of unmeaning signs, which this *person*, who was not a Mason of any degree, rightly enough conjectured were intended to blind him, and cause him to forget the *real* and true sign, which he had plainly seen with his own eyes. *But not so:* he harbored it up in his mind, and rolled it as a sweet morsel under his tongue, not that he intended any ill to the Craft, for he had always revered the Institution, but that he had got a glimpse into that mystic science which set human scrutiny at defiance: I need no longer conceal the fact, that I myself, the writer of these pages, was that person, "*not a Mason.*"

My friend of the Arch degree I saw frequently, but never hinted to him anything of the *sign*, nor, of course, he to me. I had heard before, that Masons gave signs when they met the Tyler at the door, which gained them admittance; but my chief difficulty was to ascertain to what particular degree this sign belonged. This puzzled me considerably. Things passed on for several months in this way, without putting my sign to the test; as I dare as well cut my throat as attempt to visit a Lodge or Chapter in Boston, where this man of the due-guard sign would be liable to detect me. So having some business in New York City, I thought that an excellent opportunity to try my sign, and learn if it would pass current. Accordingly, on the first night of my arrival I inquired of my landlord, if a Lodge met in the city that evening, and he told me one did, and that, too, in an upper story of the house I was in!

This rather startled me, to think I was so near the threshold, which would either gratify my eager curiosity, or perhaps, cause my disgrace; and more especially, when the landlord told me that he was then going up, and "would be happy to see me there after supper." I determined, however, to venture at all hazards, and accordingly, after supper, I groped my way up into the fourth story, as directed by the landlord, where I found the Tyler in his shirt sleeves, with a drawn sword. Never shall I forget my feelings at that instant: I would have given worlds had I remained down stairs, and held my tongue, instead of babbling to the landlord about Lodges and Masonry; but there was no backing out—the stair-way was a very narrow and strait one, and I could make no reasonable excuse, as that of having missed my way, &c. I accordingly sneaked up to the Tyler, and bidding him a good evening, which he very civilly returned, I told him I would like to visit his Lodge.

He then asked me if any Brother could vouch for me. I told him I did not know, as I was an entire stranger in the place; but I presumed *that* would satisfy him. Here I gave the due-guard sign spoken of above, and he, nearly at the same time, gave three knocks at the door, which immediately opened, and he whispered to the person who opened it, that a stranger wished to be examined, without noticing my sign in the least; and the door immediately closed.

Now the truth was, as the reader may well suppose, I did *not* wish to be examined, especially after the reception my sign had met with in the eyes of the Tyler; and I had just begun to say I believed I would call again, and had half turned round, when the door opened, and out popped three Masons with aprons on, one of whom, to my utter confusion, I instantly recognized as my landlord! "This is the gentleman," said the Tyler, "who wishes to be examined," "I believe,"—said I,—"I will call another—" "O,"—said the landlord,—"it will take but a minute;"—and by this time, rather than be suspected of being an impostor for *one* moment, I had suffered myself to be led into the private room by my *kind* landlord, for the purpose of proving myself one, the *next*.

"How many degrees have you taken?"—asked the landlord.* I here gave the due-guard sign, as well as my trembling frame would permit. Here the landlord requested one of the Brethren to leave us for a few minutes; and he had no sooner gone out, than the landlord told me that "*that* Brother *was only a Master Mason*, and that I was very indiscreet in giving that sign, without first being satisfied that all present were *Royal Arch Masons*." He then said that all was now safe, and perhaps it would be as well to examine on the Royal Arch degree at once, as it would save time. I stood motionless. At length the landlord asked, "By what rights do you claim admission?" Here I again gave the due-guard sign; and had I known enough to have first said: "*By the rights of the Royal Arch*," all had been well; but I said nothing, and stood like an aspen leaf. The two stared at each other, and at length the landlord said, "To what does that allude?" I here again, like a fool, gave the due-guard sign—and they stared at each other more than ever, and whispered to each other. ***********. At length I was *permitted* to slink down stairs, pay my bill at the bar, and depart in peace to seek new lodgings.

---

* I have since become convinced that they all, the landlord in particular, took me for a Mason; and my exposure was not their fault, but my own.

LIFE,

ABDUCTION AND MURDER

OF

WILLIAM MORGAN,

TAKEN FROM

THE PROCEEDINGS OF THE ANTI-MASONIC CONVENTION:

AND THE CONFESSION OF

HENRY L. VALANCE,

[ONE OF THE MURDERERS.]

WILLIAM MORGAN was born on the 7th day of August, 1774, in Culpepper county, Virginia. His occupation was that of a bricklayer and stone mason. Having accumulated by his industry, a sufficient fund, he commenced business as a merchant in Richmond, Virginia. It is said, that he was a captain in a militia regiment, and that he was present at the battle of New Orleans, in January, 1815. He married Lucinda Pendleton, in October, 1819, who was left with two infant children at the time of his abduction. He removed from Virginia in the fall of 1821, and commenced the business of a brewer, near York, in Upper Canada. The destruction of his property, by fire, soon after, reduced him to poverty. He removed to Rochester, in the state of New York, and resumed his original occupation. An inflammation of the eyes, contracted soon after, incapacitated him for labor, and rendered the pressure of poverty more severe. From Rochester he removed to Batavia, where he resided in the summer of 1826. William Morgan was a member of the masonic fraternity, and had advanced as far as the degree of royal arch, in the mysteries of that society. In the summer of 1826, it became known that he was preparing for publication, a work, in which the obligations, secret signs, and ceremonies of freemasonry were to be made public. It was also understood that David C. Miller, an Entered Apprentice Mason, and a printer at Batavia, was engaged, or to be engaged in printing the work. The knowledge of these facts excited great commotion, among the members of the masonic fraternity in that vicinity, and in a wide extent of surrounding country. There was great heat and intemperance of expression in relation to the expected work, and an open avowal by members, that it should never see the light. Consultations were held among them, as to the course to be pursued in relation to the contemplated work; and it was understood, finally, to have been determined, that its publication was to be prevented at all hazards. It would appear, that there were several different and distinct projects devised, to produce this result, which, either were not attempted or failed in their execution.

Arrangements were made for the assembling at Batavia, on the night of the 8th of September, of members of the masonic fraternity, from different and distant places. They came from Buffalo, Lockport, Canandaigua, and Rochester, and expectations were entertained that there would also be a party from Canada. None of them arrived at Batavia until in the night, when they assembled to the number of forty or fifty, or more. The object of this party was to suppress the publication of the work, by procuring the manuscript papers, and the printed sheets. For this purpose, an attack upon the printing office of Miller, was contemplated, and it would seem also, the forcible removal of Morgan, from Batavia, to effect a separation between him and Miller. Eli Bruce, the sheriff of Niagara county, had been requested to prepare, and did actually prepare a cell in the jail of that county, for the reception of Morgan, whose forcible abduction, by this band of midnight conspirators, was confidently expected. Colonel Edward Sawyer, of Canandaigua, headed, or commanded this party; but they failed to effect their object, and dispersed a little before daylight, the next morning.

It is supposed that they were deterred from their purpose, by a knowledge of the fact, that Miller was aware of their intentions, and had prepared fire-arms, and other ample means to defend, both his person and his property, from the attacks of violence. Many of the persons composing this party are known to have been selected and delegated for the express purpose of going to Batavia, to assist in suppressing the publication of Morgan's book; and perhaps the numbers composing this party, and the different and distant places from which they came, illustrate more forcibly than any other single fact, the extent of the combination to suppress the publication of the book.

On Sunday morning, September 10th, Nicholas G. Chesebro, of Canandaigua, master of the lodge at that place, applied to Jeffrey Chipman, a magistrate at Canandaigua, for a warrant. Chesebro came to the office with Ebenezer C. Kingsley, who made a complaint against William Morgan, for having taken away a shirt and cravat, which he had borrowed of Kingsley. The magistrate issued the warrant upon the oath of Kingsley, was directed to Chesebro, as one of the coroners of Ontario county, and handed to him. Chesebro, together with Halloway Hayward, a constable, Henry Howard, Harris Seymour, Moses Roberts, and Joseph Scofield, all freemasons, of Canandaigua, left that place for Batavia, at about ten o'clock the same morning, in an extra stage, hired by Chesebro.

The party were joined by four other individuals, all freemasons, at different places, before they reached Batavia. They stopped to take supper at James Ganson's house, in Stafford, six miles east of Batavia. Dr. Samuel S. Butler, of Stafford, was then introduced to some of the party, and informed that they had a warrant for Morgan. Doctor Butler went to Batavia the same evening, and was requested to inform Nathan Follett, and William Seaver, then master of the Batavia lodge, that the party were coming. He did so, and on his return met the Canandaigua party about two miles from Batavia, and informed Ganson that Follett had sent to them not to come. The stage turned about; the party that originally started from Canandaigua went into Batavia on foot, and the remainder returned. The next morning early, Morgan was arrested, and taken to the public house where the party had slept; an extra stage coach was procured, and the party left Batavia for Canandaigua, with Morgan in their custody. Miller attempted to procure the release of Morgan, just as the carriage was starting, but he was pushed aside, and the coach was driven off very fast, Chesebro being on the outside with the driver, and urging him to drive fast, until they should get out of the county. The driver appeared to feel uneasy about the proceedings, but was pacified by Ganson's assurance, that he would save him harmless from all responsibility. Chesebro repeatedly looked back, and said they should not take Morgan alive. They arrived at Canandaigua with Morgan the same day, and in the evening took him before the magistrate, who issued the warrant, by whom he was examined and discharged, Loton Lawson appearing as a witness on behalf of Morgan. Chesebro then immediately applied to the same magistrate for a warrant against Morgan, for a debt of about two dollars, claimed to be due from him to Aaron Ackley, a tavern keeper, which debt Chesebro alleged, was assigned to him. Judgment was entered against Morgan, for two dollars and sixty-nine cents, debt and costs, and an execution immediately issued, which was put into the hands of Halloway Hayward, then present. Morgan took off his coat, and offered it to the constable to levy upon, for the debt. The constable declined receiving it, and arrested Morgan and committed him to the jail of Canandaigua the same evening, on the execution. He remained in custody, in Canandaigua jail, until the evening of the next day.

Immediately after Morgan was committed to jail, Loton Lawson, a farmer residing near Canandaigua, procured a horse and went to Rochester the same night, a distance of twenty-eight miles, and returned the next morning a little after breakfast. He went to bed soon after his return, and informed the innkeeper where he slept, that some gentleman from Rochester would call for him in the course of the day. On the 12th of September, Burrage Smith, and John Whitney, of Rochester, took the stage from that place in the morning, for Canandaigua. They were joined by James Gillis, at Victor, ten miles distant from Canandaigua, and all three arrived at the latter place early in the afternoon of the same day. Smith and Whitney called upon Loton Lawson, in the evening of the same day, September 12; Loton Lawson called at the jail a little after dark, and asked for William Morgan. The jailer was absent, and Lawson informed the jailer's wife, that he wished to pay the debt for which Morgan was confined, and take him away. Mrs. Hall (the jailer's wife,), declined accepting the amount of the execution, on the ground that she did not know the amount, and also refused to permit Lawson to have any private conversation with Morgan. Lawson asked Morgan, however, in the presence of Mrs. Hall, if he would go home with him if he would pay the debt and take him out? To which Morgan answered that he would; Lawson then expressed great anxiety to get Morgan out that night, and pressed Mrs. Hall to receive the amount of the debt, which she still declined.

Lawson went out and returned soon with another person whom Mrs. Hall cannot identify, and insisted on her receiving the amount of the execution. Mrs. Hall peremptorily refused. He went away and returned again, reiterating his request with the same effect. He went away again, and soon returned with Edward Sawyer, who advised Mrs. Hall to receive the amount of the debt, and let Morgan go. She still refused. She subsequently consented to discharge Morgan, at the requst of Nicholas G. Chesebro, who was the real plaintiff in the execution, and took the keys of the prison for the purpose of opening Morgan's cell. Before she opened the cell, Lawson gave a single whistle at the front door, which brought a man to the jail steps. Morgan's cell was unlocked; he came out, and Lawson took him by his arm, and went toward the door of the prison hall, which was unlocked by a person on the outside, and they went out. Before they left the jail steps, Morgan was seized with violence, by Lawson, and the person who was called there by his whistle. Morgan struggled and cried 'murder' once or twice, resisting as much as possible, and in the struggle his hat fell off. Edward Sawyer, and Nicholas G. Chesebro, were waiting near the jail steps, and when the struggle commenced, they followed Morgan and the two men who were with him, and who were going eastwardly from the jail. Chesebro came up with them and stopped Morgan's outcry, by thrusting a handkerchief, or something similar, into his mouth. Sawyer gave a distinct rap upon the curb of a well, at which signal, Hiram Hubbard drove up with a two horse carriage, which had been harnessed, and was in waiting for the purpose. He overtook the party, having Morgan in their possession, a few rods east of the jail, when two of them thrust Morgan into the carriage, and then got in themselves. The carriage immediately turned around, and drove through Canandaigua, Main street, northerly. This was about nine o'clock in the evening, and it was a bright moonlight night. Loton Lawson, Burrage Smith, John Whitney, James Gillis, and probably one or two other persons, whose names are not known, either rode in, or accompanied, the carriage containing Morgan. It would seem, that this carriage was accompanied most of the distance by out-riders, either on horseback, or in some separate conveyance. A sulky, with a man in it, started from Canandaigua just after the carriage drove through the street, for which it appeared to have been waiting some time; it drove past the carriage about three miles from Canandaigua, and stopped at Victor over-night. At Victor, the carriage containing Morgan, and the party with him, drove into Enos Gillis' yard, back of his barn, and out of sight of the road; and the party remained there about an hour, and took some refreshments. James Gillis here took a horse from his brother's stable, and it would also seem, that one other of the party accompanied or preceded the carriage, on horseback, when it left Victor. On the morning of the 13th of September, between four and five o'clock, Ezra Platt, a livery stable keeper, in Rochester, and a Royal Arch Mason, was called upon for a carriage to go to Lewistown, and requested it to be sent to Ensworth's tavern, in the village. He called up Orson Parkhurst, one of his drivers, who is also a Mason, and directed him to prepare the carriage. Platt charged the hire of the carriage, as he has sworn, to "The Grand Chapter, pro tem." He has not yet received his pay for such a singular charge.

The carriage containing Morgan, and the party with him, drove into Rochester about day-dawn, and Hubbard watered his horse at the public reservoir, near the center of the village. He has testified that one individual alighted from the carriage here, and was absent about fifteen minutes, when the same person returned, as he supposed. The carriage then drove north, about three miles from Rochester, where the ridge road turns off from the river road. It stopped at the tavern at the intersection of the roads a short time, with the intention of feeding. For some reason this intention was abandoned, and Hubbard drove the carriage about half a mile from the tavern, on the ridge road, and set down the whole party in the road, at a distance from any house, and near a piece of wood. The curtains of this carriage, so far as it had been seen by day-light, were closed. After Hubbard had set his party down, he returned, with the curtains of his carriage rolled up. Soon after the carriage left the tavern, going west, Edward Doyle, of Rochester, rode up, on a horse belonging to Ezra Platt, and inquired if such a carriage had passed, and which way it went. Being informed, he followed after it. Platt's carriage, driven by Orson Parkhurst, with some individuals in it, soon drove on the same road. It took up the party that Hubbard had left in the road, or a portion of them, with Morgan, and drove west. Edward Doyle, on horseback, and four or five persons in Hubbard's carriage, returned to Rochester.

A gentleman of Clarkson had engaged a pair of horses of Silas Walbridge, of that place, to put before a carriage. The carriage driven by Parkhurst drove up to Clarkson about nine o'clock in the morning, with the curtains and windows closed, though it was a warm day. This is about fifteen miles west of the place where Parkhurst took in his party. Upon its arrival in the street of Clarkson, the gentleman who had engaged Walbridge's horses, told him that he should not want them, and immediately got into his sulky, and drove about two and a half miles further west, and engaged a pair of horses of one Captain Isaac Allen, a farmer. The carriage did not stop in Clarkson, but drove on to Allen's. Upon its arrival, Allen's horses were taken out of the orchard where they had been drawing apples, and were harnessed to the carriage which Parkhurst drove, in exchange for the horses which he had before driven, and Parkhurst mounted the box again and drove on west. When the carriage arrived at Gaines, about fifteen miles west of Clarkson, Elihu Mather, residing at that place, took the horses of his brother, James Mather, and followed the carriage, which had passed west through the village. He overtook it at some distance from the village, where the horses were exchanged in the street, at a distance from any house. When the exchange was effected, Elihu Mather himself got upon the box, and drove the carriage west, while Parkhurst returned east with Allen's horses.

The stage which had left Rochester early the same morning, arrived at Murdoch's tavern before the carriage containing Morgan passed. A gentleman of high standing, of Rochester, was one of the passengers in the stage; when the stage arrived at Murdoch's tavern, this gentleman called the man aside who then had charge of the tavern, and asked him if he was a Royal Arch Mason; being answered in the negative, he asked for writing materials, with which he wrote a note, and dispatched a boy with it to Jeremiah Brown, residing in that vicinity. Jeremiah Brown came to the tavern soon after, and held a conversation with him. When the stage went on, Brown and the gentleman both went on in it. Soon after, Brown returned to the tavern with two horses, riding one and leading the other. When the carriage containing Morgan came along, which was soon after, Elihu Mather, who was then driving it, beckoned to Brown after the carriage had passed the house a short distance, and Brown went up to him, and appeared to hold some conversation with him. The carriage drove on, Brown took his horses, and followed on after it; but it would seem that he left his horses, and got on to the carriage himself. Burrage Smith had followed the Morgan carriage in a sulky, but he had not overtaken it when the carriage arrived at Murdoch's. The carriage stopped that evening at the tavern of Solomon C. Wright, in New Fane, Niagara county, where the road turns off to

Lockport, and about three miles distant therefrom. It was here driven into the barn, and the doors closed, and the party remained at this place some time, to procure refreshments, and to make arrangements for relieving those who had traveled in the carriage with Morgan all day, and the whole of the previous night, and who must necessarily have been greatly fatigued.

Burrage Smith went to Lockport in his sulky, and, together with Jared Darrow, called upon Eli Bruce, the sheriff of Niagara county, and informed him that Morgan was in their possession, and was going to Canada, and requested Bruce's assistance in getting him along. Bruce and some others went to Wright's, where several persons were assembled. Bruce and David Hague got into the carriage with Morgan; Elihu Mather drove and Jeremiah Brown was on the box with him, and they left Wright's about ten o'clock in the evening. The persons who came there with Morgan, probably most of them went to Lockport that night, and went into Lewistown the next day in a stage coach. At Molyneux's tavern, six miles distant, they stopped, and Bruce procured Molyneux's horses in exchange for Mather's. An individual accompanied the carriage on horseback. Brown then drove, and they reached Lewistown, fourteen miles distant from Molyneux's, somewhat after midnight. The carriage was driven around to a back street, and unharnessed. Samuel Burton, one of the proprietors of the stage line at Lewistown, was called upon for assistance. He called up Corydon Fox, one of his drivers, and directed him to harness a carriage. He did so, and drove up to the tavern. Bruce got upon the box with him, and by his direction Fox drove around to the back street, where the other carriage was unharnessed, when Morgan was taken out of the one carriage and put into the carriage which Fox drove. Bruce and Hague got in with him, and Fox, by Bruce's direction, drove to Youngstown. They called at the house of Col. William King, at Youngstown, and stopped. Bruce alighted, and called up King, who came out with Bruce, and both got into the carriage. Fox drove on toward the fort, by Bruce's direction, and when arrived at the burying-ground near the fort, he was told to stop. He did so, when the persons having Morgan in charge got out, together with Morgan, and all four walked off, arm in arm, toward the fort, and Fox was told he might return. Morgan was hoodwinked and bound at this time. It appears that arrangements had been previously made for the reception of Morgan upon the Crv-ada side of the river, with persons residing upon that side.

CONFESSIONS

OF

HENRY L. VALANCE.

It is from the time of the arrival at the Fort of Niagara, that my connection with this unhappy business more particularly dates. Up to the time of which I am now speaking, I had not been more concerned in it than others   But, from some cause or other, the more daring of the American conspirators, who had resolved in their hearts to go all lengths in the awful path on which they had entered, should it be necessary for their safety so to do—these men, I say, selected me and some few other of the Canadians, as persons upon whom they could most rely in the event of their resorting to extremities. They took us into their confidence in a very marked manner, and the consequence was a degree of intimacy far greater than would have followed from the ordinary masonic tie. We discussed the whole matter, in all its bearings, and the death of the offender was darkly and obscurely hinted at in our nocturnal consultations. It did not, however, assume other than a shadowy shape, and the crime itself would have remained unperpetrated, had it not been that we had placed ourselves in a position where a feather's weight was sufficient to turn the scale against the life of the victim of a mistaken view of our masonic obligations. Circumstances, in themselves trivial, led to the death, rather than the continued confinement or banishment of Morgan, as I shall now proceed to show.

Morgan, as all the world knows, had been confined in the magazine of Fort Niagara. The keeper of the Fort was a Mason, and a man upon whom we could most confidently rely, as he had entered heart and soul into the plan of abduction, and was ready to go as far as the worst of us for the purpose of preventing Morgan's disclosures, or for punishing a traitor, as we all held Morgan to be. Had he been alone there, all would have gone as well as the most lenient of our number could have desired; but his wife was with him, and it was through her conduct that we felt ourselves compelled to silence him who could have borne testimony against us had he managed to obtain his freedom. This woman came to the knowledge of the fact that some one was confined illegally in the fort, and she demanded to be made acquainted with the whole circumstances of the transaction in which we were engaged. Her husband not only refused to comply with her request, in the dread that it would lead to the discovery of the entire matter, and the arrest and severe punishment of all the parties to it; but he endeavored to enforce silence upon her. This, of course, she being a spirited woman, only rendered things worse. Dispute followed dispute, and one quarrel trod fast on the heels of another, until the wife finally left her husband, and returned for protection to the house of her father. To her father she communicated the cause of those domestic dissensions which had led to the separation from her husband. He was struck with her narrative, and determined, after considerable reflection, to see his son-in-law, and to demand an explanation of the mysterious circumstance rather than make a public affair of what, after all, might prove to be but one of those difficulties which occasionally occur in married life. He said nothing to his daughter however, of his intended course of action, but proceeded to the fort, and saw his son-in-law. There was much composure in the manner of the latter when the subject was broached, and he endeavored to give such a coloring to his matrimonial difficulties as would, had he succeeded, have placed the inquirer on a wrong scent. But his very manner was sufficient to give the lie to the part he was attempting to perform in so unskillful a way; and the old man probed him so deeply as to almost penetrate to the details of the whole business. Had he done so, how much better would it have been for poor Morgan! and still how much better would it have been for his murderers!

The result of the father-in-law's inquiries amounted to this, that some one was illegally confined in the Fort, but who he was, or for what purpose imprisoned, he could not ascertain. He then told the keeper, that he would give him twenty-four hours in which to release the man, and if within that time he should not be released, resort would be had to legal means to restore him to the enjoyment of freedom. It was his duty to have insisted upon his immediate liberation, and that duty would have probably been performed had not the keeper been so nearly connected with him, his wish being to prevent his relative from suffering the consequences of his conduct, provided he should at last act in accordance with the dictates of justice. I should have mentioned, that the keeper's father-in-law was not a mason, and therefore the keeper could not confide to him either the name of his prisoner or the cause of his incarceration.

As soon as his father-in-law had left him, the keeper proceeded to notify us of the nature of the interview he had had with his relative. He plainly told us that something must be done immediately, and that if Morgan was not disposed of before the next morning, not only should we all be arrested and severely punished, but that there would be a great excitement raised against the order, and that it would fall before the torrent of popular indignation, suffering more severely than it could have done had Morgan's book been published, and allowed to pass without question. It needed not that he should tell us this, for it was self-evident to every man in the dark and agitated company. A long and serious consultation took place. Many plans were proposed, discussed, and rejected in their turn, having for their object the removal of our prisoner to some more secure place of confinement: for it was difficult to settle upon a place less likely to be disturbed than that which had been originally selected. The fort had been selected, at the start, because it was supposed that it combined in a superior degree the leading essentials of a secret prison; yet this deeply contrived plan had been baffled by so simple and common place a thing as the curiosity of a woman! What security could we have that any other prison would prove a better retainer of its secrets? Such security was not to be had and we saw before us the prospect of continued danger, a constant dread of detection and punishment, to say nothing of the danger to our order, so long as Morgan should live. Our liberty, our property, our characters, and the **great** institution in whose behalf we had originally undertaken to act, would all, for very many years, it was probable, be at the mercy of every woman or child who should chance to be in the vicinity of our victim's prison.

It was while we were in this state of doubt and uncertainty, regretting the past and trembling for the future, that one of our number rose to speak. He was a thoughtful, silent man, generally, but always ready to act when anything was to be done, and had the reputation among us of being more deeply concerned in the business of kidnapping Morgan than any other of the conspirators. "Brethren," he said, in a firm voice, "there is no denying that our situation is a most critical one; but it is the characteristic of determined, resolute men, that they always rise superior to those difficulties which are fatal to the weak and vacillating. If we are firm, and do not allow ourselves to be deterred from pursuing the only course, that can lead to safety, all will yet be well with us. What have we to fear? It is, that Morgan may recover his liberty, and bring down upon our heads the whole weight of the law, and put our order under the ban of public opinion, against which no institution, however strong, can maintain itself. How are these difficulties to be avoided? To me it seems clear that they can be avoided only by consigning Morgan to that confinement from which alone there is no possibility of escape—THAT OF THE GRAVE! This may appear to some of you a dread alternative, but I have been prepared for it from the beginning, as the probable result of this man's seizure and imprisonment. Nor will there be anything so decidedly unjust in our thus disposing of him. Has he not placed himself in the position of a traitor; and have not the laws of God and man, in all ages, condemned traitors to suffer in full the last penalty? And what is the treachery which directs itself only against a country or a king, in comparison with that which aims at the overthrow of a vast institution which is gathering into its folds men of every country, and binding all mankind into a common brotherhood? I say, that Morgan has incurred the penalty of death, and that to visit that penalty upon him will be an act of justice, and according to the principles that prevail among men in all forms of society. Our own safety, too, points to the same course; and, for one, I am ready to bear a full part in placing him in the only prison that can make us all safe, while at the same time it will be a just punishment of his treachery."

The words of a bold man, in times of doubt and trial, are always effectual. They were so in the present case, and the greater part of the company were carried away by the speech of the daring American. They assented at once to the force of his arguments, and avowed their readiness to aid him in any measure that he should deem proper under the circumstances. Some few were silent, and neither approved nor condemned the sentiments that had been put forth; and from this position they were as deeply involved, and as guilty, as those who were most forward in their desire for the shedding of blood. Before we separated, the death of Morgan was fully resolved upon; and it was agreed to meet on the evening of that day, and fix upon the mode of EXECUTION.

In the evening we all met. Several plans for putting our prisoner to death were proposed, but that which was finally adopted came from the same man who had been so successful in convincing us that we should proceed to extremities. We were eight in number, and it was determined that three of us should be selected by lot to perform the part of executioners. Eight pieces of paper were procured, five of which were to remain blank, while the letter D was written on the others. These pieces of paper were placed in a large box, from which each man was to draw one at the same moment. After drawing, we were all to separate, without looking at the paper that each held in his hand. So soon as we had arrived at certain distances from the place of rendezvous, the tickets were to be examined, and those who held blanks were to return instantly to their homes; and those three who should hold the marked tickets were to proceed to the Fort at midnight, and there put Morgan to death, in such a manner as should seem to themselves most fitting. The tickets were placed in the box, and drawn forth simultaneously, and we all left the place, in different directions, without looking at our papers. The proceeding was so rapid, that I had no time for reflection until I found myself in the open air; and walking fast to a point at which I thought it would be safe for me to examine my ticket; and even then I did not think so much of the atrocious nature of the crime in which I was engaged, as of the chances that there were of my having drawn a blank, which would indeed have been a prize to me. After walking for a mile or thereabouts, and seeing that no one was near, I halted, and examined my ticket, which I had kept within my clenched hand. I started back with horror, as, by the dim light, I was enabled to trace the fatal letter, distinctly drawn on the white ground! My first thought was to turn and fly, but where should I fly to? Would not my comrades suspect the cause of my absence, and would they not, from regard to their own safety, deem it necessary to treat me as they were about to treat Morgan? Beside, was I not bound in honor—aye, and by my oath, too—to go onward in the enterprise, horrible and unlawful as it was, and fearful as might be its consequences? I had offered no remonstrances against the plan for the making away with Morgan, but had gone on, step by step, with the other conspirators; and was I not, therefore, bound in honor to continue in the same fearful path unto the end? Strange as it may appear, and so singularly is the mind of man constituted, the sensation that I most deeply experienced at that awful moment, was one of shame, that I should have thought of evading the dread task that I had been selected by fortune to perform. All idea of its criminality was absorbed in this, and I resolved to go through with the enterprise with a bold heart and a steady hand.

As the hour for the meeting of the three approached, I proceeded toward the Fort, not without a lingering hope that the two who were to be associated with me as executioners, would be less punctual than myself, and that they would fail altogether of keeping their rendezvous. But this hope soon left me, for as I arrived near the Fort, I was joined by two of those from whom I had so recently separated, and then it was that we ascertained who had drawn the death-tickets. Both these men were Americans, and neither of them, I am certain, had less desire to take any part in the affair than myself. However, there was now no show of reluctance, all of us acting as if we had made up our minds to the performance of a terrible task, from which there was no retreat. Immediate arrangements were made to carry out the sentence, if such it can be called, that had been passed upon the prisoner. My comrades left to procure a boat, one of them knowing where it was easy to find it, it having been agreed upon that Morgan should be sunk in the Niagara, in hope that he and our crime alike would thus be buried beneath the waves. My part was to proceed to the magazine, and announce to Morgan his fate, and to prepare him, so far as I could, to meet it.

When my partners in crime had left, I passed to the magazine. On entering, I found Morgan asleep, and for a few moments I stood and regarded him by the light of the lantern that I had brought with me. He was pale and haggard, and looked like an old man, though in reality he was not much past the prime of existence. Nevertheless, he slept quietly, and my entrance did not appear to have disturbed him. I gently awoke him, and he started wildly up, and gazed upon me. I was a stranger to him, and he hurriedly demanded my business. "William Morgan," I replied, "I come to you on a sad duty—it is to prepare you for your last hour on earth. The great crime of which you have been guilty, has been duly considered by those against whom it has been committed; and they, possessed both of the right and the power to act, have resolved that you must die. It is now past midnight, and before the earliest dawn shall have appeared, you must be no longer on earth. I leave you to prepare for the great change you are to undergo." Thus saying, I placed the lantern on the floor, and was in the act of leaving the magazine, for the purpose of stationing myself at the entrance, when Morgan loudly called me back, and poured out a number of questions. He demanded by what authority we had condemned him? who had been his judges? were they Americans or foreigners? how was he to die? and many other questions of the like character. I told him that I had not come there to answer questions, but to notify him of his sentence, from which there was no appeal, or possibility of escape. I added, that I had heard he had been a soldier, that I had been one myself, and that I hoped he would meet his end as became a man who had borne arms. He took no notice of this, but commenced wringing his hands, and talking of his wife and children, the recollection of whom in that awful hour terribly affected him. His wife, he said, was young and inexperienced, and his children were but infants; what would become of them were he, the husband and father, cut off, and they even ignorant of his fate? I endeavored to console him on this point, by assuring him that the fraternity of which he had been an unworthy member, and which he had sought to ruin, had already provided for his family, and that they would not be permitted to want anything. He then commenced a rambling discourse, and begged to know if there was no avoiding his fate, promising to give up all his papers, to go to any part of the world we might send him, and there reside, seeking to have no communication with America, and living a different life from that he had formerly pursued—by which I understood that he would maintain his Masonic obligations. Just as I was about to reply to him, my comrades came to the door of the magazine, which they opened, and beckoned me to come to them, which I did. They informed me that they had procured a boat and a number of heavy weights, and that everything was ready on their part, and demanded to know if Morgan himself was prepared. Before I could answer Morgan commenced shouting, as if in the hope of obtaining assistance. "By God!" said one of our number, "THAT must be stopped, or we may yet all be discovered!" So saying he entered the Magazine, followed by myself and ———; and striding up to Morgan, he bade him cease that useless alarm, which could avail him nothing, for that die he must, if we had to kill him where he stood. As if cowed by the fierceness of this demonstration, Morgan stopped shouting, and again began remonstrating against our conduct, which he declared to be wholly unjustifiable, even if he had violated his masonic obligations, for Masons had no right to put men to death. He was again told that all remonstrances were idle, and that he should prepare himself for death, otherwise he would have to die without making his peace. From this moment, and as if his nature revolted against the oppression of which he was the object, his bearing underwent a change. He became more firm, and disdained to make further appeals for mercy for himself, but the feelings of the husband and the father were still strong within him, and he humbled himself so far as to plead in behalf of his family. He begged that some permanent provision might be made for them, and, above all things, implored us to communicate his fate to his wife. He requested that one of us would write a letter to his wife, making her acquainted with the facts connected with his death, in order that her mind might be relieved from the horrors of uncertainty. As we saw no harm in making this promise, which of course we had no idea of keeping, we pledged ourselves to comply with his request, and assured him that his family should not be permitted to suffer from poverty. We then told him that we would leave him alone for half an hour, at the end of which time we should expect to find him prepared to meet his inevitable fate. He merely bowed, by way of reply.

Retiring from the room, we stationed ourselves near the door, and endeavored to prevent reflection by conversation carried on in a low tone. But it was in vain, every effort was a failure; and at last, a gloomy silence fell over us, which none ventured to disturb. How Morgan passed the time, I cannot say. Everything was quiet as the tomb within. As he was chained and handcuffed, he could not move without our hearing him—and not the faintest sound fell upon our ears, which were so painfully open to everything, that I verily believe the falling of a leaf in our midst would have caused us to start with terror. Most probably he indulged in that rapid reflection which is always caused by the certainty of the fast approach of death; and his whole life, with its mingled pictures of good and ill, passed before his fervid vision. Perhaps he prayed, not only for himself and his family, but for his murderers. But I cannot dwell upon the subject, which, even at this distance of time, appals the memory.

The time having expired, we entered the magazine, and found Morgan ready to receive us. He made no remonstrances, nor offered any resistance, his demeanor and acts being in all respects those of a man who has nerved himself boldly to meet a certain doom. We bound his hands behind him, and placed a gag in his mouth. One of our number marched a few yards in advance, and was followed by myself and the other associate, between whom walked Morgan. We each had hold of one of his arms, above the elbow. A short time brought us to where the boat had been placed, and we all entered it, Morgan being placed in the bows, with myself alongside of him. My comrades took the oars, and the boat was rapidly forced out into the river. The night was pitch dark, and we could scarcely see a yard before us, and therefore was the time admirably adapted to our hellish purpose. Having arrived at a place sufficiently removed from the land, the rowers ceased from their labors, and my particular duty now commenced. In the bottom of the boat lay a number of heavy weights, all tied together by a strong cord, that had been carried through the ring of each weight, so that they formed one mass. From the center of the cord by which they were united, proceeded another cord, of equal strength, and several yards in length. This cord I took in my hand, and fastened it around the body of Morgan, just above his hips, using all my skill to make it fast, so that it would hold. Then, in a whisper, I bade the unhappy man to stand up, and after a momentary hesitation, he complied with my order. He stood close to the head of the boat, and there was just length enough of rope from his person to the weights to prevent any strain, while he was standing. I then requested one of my associates to assist me in lifting the weights from the bottom to the side of the boat, while the other steadied her from the stern. This was done, and, as Morgan was standing with his back toward me, and apparently looking into the water, I approached him, and gave him a strong push with both my hands, which were placed on the middle of his back. He fell forward, carrying the weights with him, and the waters closed over the mass. We remained quiet for the space of two or three minutes, when my companions, without saying a word, resumed their places, and rowed the boat to the place from which they had taken it. We then jumped ashore, and, exchanging pressures of the hand, separated without a word.

I made my way home with all dispatch, trembling at every sound, and dreading at each moment that I should meet some one who might recognize me, notwithstanding the blackness of darkness in which the earth was enshrouded. So great were my fears for my personal safety, that I did not reflect on the villany in which I had been engaged, by which a fellow-creature had been deprived of life, and a family bereft of its protector. It was not until I had managed to reach my bed-room without falling in with any one, that reflection came; and from that hour must I date the commencement of those torments which have never since left me. I threw myself on my bed, but sleep would not visit me. I was in a state of nervous excitement, and began to experience the gnawings of the worm that never dies, and to feel the intensity of the fire that is never quenched. At the earliest dawn I rose, and went out and wandered forth among the forests, tortured by remorse, and cursing the folly that had led me to imbrue my hands in Morgan's blood. For some days I continued in the vicinity, but at last I determined to go into the States, for the purpose of getting away from the scene of my crime. I proceeded to that part of New York in which the anti-Masonic excitement originated, and was an apparently calm spectator of the evils that grew out of the intense and just indignation of a people stirred to their inmost souls by the occurrence of a mysterious crime, that had baffled the law, and whose perpetrators seemed to be as much above the reach of ordinary human power as were the members of the once terrible Secret Tribunal of Germany. I remained there for a considerable length of time, as if fascinated; and I not only attended anti-Masonic meetings, but likewise many of the trials that grew out of the Morgan outrage.

The excited state of the public mind was in unison with my own feelings, which could not settle down into a condition of calmness. No man in that part of the world was acquainted with the part I had played in the murder of Morgan, for it may easily be believed that I would not take any one into my confidence; and of those who had been concerned in the affair with me, either in consultation or action, none resided near to my then place of abode. Of my fellow-executioners, both had absented themselves from their homes within a very short space of time after that fatal night; nor have I any reason for supposing that either of them ever communicated the fact of my having been united with them in the deed of murder, to third parties. If it should be asked why I did not unburthen my mind to brother Masons, my reply is, that, in the first place, I thought I had no right to render them accessories to my crime, as by such confidence they would in a certain sense have become; and when I saw Masons, who for a long time had breasted the storm, leaving and undermining the order, either from conscientious or interested motives, it occurred to me that I should endanger my life by taking any man into my confidence. Thus being compelled to retain the dread secret in my bosom, my existence became to the last degree miserable, and my health so declined that I began to fear I should soon be called upon to render an account to a greater power than that of any earthly tribunal, and from whose scrutiny no secret could be concealed. Though my life was a burthen, I did not the less dread death, for I could not bring my mind to the belief that with the grave there comes annihilation and accountability ceases. I shunned society, and passed all the hours that were at my command in solitude, a change having come over my thoughts; and as at first I sought all public places, and crowds were my delight, now the forest was better to me than the street, and the presence of men my abhorrence. It seemed to me as if my secret were known to all men, and that for reasons to them good they allowed of the postponement of my certain punishment. I could not walk erect, nor obtain rest, nor find pleasure in any of those pursuits in which the innocent pass their hours of leisure; and I might have been addressed in the words of the greatest of poets,—

"——————What is't that takes from thee
Thy comfort, pleasure, and thy golden sleep?
Why dost thou bend thine eyes upon the earth,
And start so often when thou sitt'st alone?
Why hast thou lost the fresh blood in thy cheek?
Oh! what portents are these?"

After remaining in western New York between two and three years, it occurred to me that change of scene might tend to relieve my mind from the weight that oppressed it, I proceeded to one of the new territories, where I resided for a considerable length of time, seeking refuge from thought and reflection in the hazards and discomforts of a frontier life. But it was all of no avail. Go where I would, or do what I would, it was impossible for me to throw off the consciousness of crime. If the mark of Cain was not upon me, the curse of the first murderer was on my soul. The blood-stain was on my hands, and could not be washed out. The avenger of blood seemed ever on my track. The remonstrances of my victim fell upon my ear, at all times and in every place. I heard them in calm and amid the storm—they whispered to me among the grass of the prairies and through the leaves of the forest. Neither change of place nor change of pursuit brought me consolation or rest. It mattered not whether I was among crowds of men, or in the silence of some wood that never before had been penetrated by civilized man; the voice of the avenger was ever sounding in my ear, and giving me to know the truth of the declaration, that mischief shall haunt the violent man!

I wandered about the north-west for many years. Had fortune been my object, I should have succeeded in obtaining it, more than one opportunity for great worldly advancement having been placed within my reach, as if to tantalize me with the sight of things that offer to other men so much pleasure, but which could not be otherwise than worthless in my jaundiced vision. I could not abide long in one place, but felt condemned to wander up and down on the face of the earth, a restless spirit, to whom is denied the enjoyment of all that men hold dear. There have been periods when I have thought of suicide, as the best means of ESCAPING FROM MYSELF; but from self-murder I have been impelled by that "fear of something after death," which "doth make cowards of us all." But it is impossible for any human power forever to continue the suffering that it has fallen to my lot to experience; and now, many years after the perpetration of the crime that destroyed my peace, far from the land of my birth, among strangers, and at the very outpost of civilization, I find death enveloping me in his cold embrace. Though I cannot otherwise than shiver at his touch, and dread what must follow from his triumph over me, my end will be to myself a release.

I have made this confession in the hope that good may flow from it, and to relieve my mind from a burden under which it has long been depressed. I have endeavored to be plain and simple in my narrative, and have not sought to harrow up the imagination of the reader. If I have not introduced the names of others into my account of an event that once was of consequence enough to excite a nation, it is because I have not wished to create prejudice against those who were connected with my associates, but who were not associated with their criminal proceedings. Whether my story will have any effect on the public mind, I know not; nor do I care. Now that years have elapsed since the abduction and murder of Morgan, people are capable of forming a righteous judgment respecting that great crime, and they no longer blindly involve the innocent in the condemnation with the guilty.

I have done. Reader, have charity on me, and remember that you have not been tempted as I was. Criminal as I am, I am also a heart-stricken penitent, and have been made to exist, as it were, on a gibbet of our own erection.